Sinners in the Hands of an Angry God

Sinners in the Hands of an Angry God

Vinu V Das

TP
Tabor Press

ISBN 978-1-997541-18-9

Table of Contents

Chapter 1. The Terrible Majesty of Divine Wrath

The sermon that shocked colonial congregations into sobbing intercession still unnerves modern hearts because it addresses something our secular age has tried to forget—God's capacity to burn with holy anger. A universe governed only by sentimental benevolence could not explain either the tragedy carved into human history or the yearning for moral reckoning embedded in every conscience. Divine wrath is not a blemish on God's character but the blazing edge of His uncompromising goodness, the necessary counterpart to perfect love in a fallen cosmos. What follows is an extended meditation on that fearful attribute, not to paint God as an arbitrary tyrant but to reveal the majesty that presses sinners toward refuge in Christ. By tracing biblical scenes, historic voices, psychological insights, and pastoral imperatives, this chapter seeks to restore awe where apathy has settled and thereby prepare the soul for the joyous news of salvation. Let the reader approach with humility, for we are handling a fire that cannot be quenched and a holiness that will not be mocked.

Prelude - A Vision That Silences Boasting

The prophet Isaiah's temple encounter (Isa 6:1-5) demonstrates how even the most righteous among mortals disintegrate under a single glimpse of unfiltered glory. While angelic attendants proclaimed "holy, holy, holy," the massive thresholds quaked, and smoke concealed the blinding brilliance that would otherwise have ended Isaiah's life instantly. This scene shows that the fear of God precedes any fruitful knowledge of Him; the heart that has never trembled cannot genuinely rejoice. Early American revivalists understood this principle, arranging their meetings so Scripture, song, and solemn silence heightened expectation before the preacher mounted the pulpit. Jonathan Edwards himself read his sermon in a measured monotone, yet eyewitnesses record that congregants clutched the wooden pillars, convinced the earth was opening beneath them. Such reactions were not mere emotional manipulation but the eruption of conscience long suppressed by outward piety. True awe strips away the fig leaves of self-approval and leaves the sinner exposed to the eyes of Him with whom we have to do (Heb 4:12-13). Only then can grace be perceived as astonishing rather than obligatory.

1.1 Scripture's Portrait of God's Anger

1.1.1 Sinai's Thundering Peaks (Ex 19–20)

Thunder, lightning, and a trumpet blast that grew louder with no human hand upon it clothed Mount Sinai when the covenant Lord descended. The mountain burned with fire to the heart of heaven, and even beasts that approached the border were to be stoned (Ex 19:12-13). God's self-disclosure was so terrifying that the liberated Israelites begged Moses to speak in His stead lest they die (Ex 20:18-19). This intensity highlights that moral law is not a negotiable social contract but the personal expression of the Creator's nature. The Ten Commandments did not float down as gentle suggestions but thundered into human history accompanied by seismic warning: grace does not dilute holiness. Sinai therefore remains a standing indictment of every generation that crafts a tame deity. The smoke and quake remind us that the One who forbids idolatry cannot Himself be turned into an idol of benevolence without righteousness. Thus the very context of divine legislation is itself part of the revelation; law and wrath are inseparable faces of covenant commitment, not contrary moods.

1.1.2 Floodwaters and Flaming Cities (Gen 6; 19)

Before the deluge, the earth was filled with violence, but the language of Genesis 6:6-7 daringly speaks of God's heart grieving—a sorrow that erupts as judgment. The global flood is not mere meteorological catastrophe but a moral reset testifying that unchecked evil will not become the final word. Similarly, Sodom and Gomorrah perished beneath sulfuric rain because their outcry reached heaven (Gen 19:13); the destruction turned fertile valley into desolate salt, a geographic sermon echoing still. Both narratives emphasize that God's patience has a terminus; accumulated rebellion eventually tips the scales. These events also reveal wrath as measured, not capricious: Noah found favor, and Lot was rescued, illustrating mercy preserved within judgment. The New Testament later employs these episodes as prototypes of eschatological certainty (2 Pet 2:5-7). Thus pre-exilic history is already eschatology in miniature, warning and assuring simultaneously.

1.1.3 Prophetic Storms: Nahum, Zephaniah, Habakkuk

The minor prophets specialize in graphic depictions of divine indignation, each tailored to specific national sins. Nahum likens God's fury against Nineveh to a whirlwind that pulverizes rocks (Nah 1:5-6), portraying judgment as a natural outflow of His character. Zephaniah announces a coming day when the Lord will sweep away everything, hinting at cosmic de-creation (Zeph 1:2-3). Habakkuk, wrestling with Judah's corruption, learns that God's "pure eyes" cannot look on evil without action (Hab 1:13). These oracles dismantle any notion that wrath belongs only to primitive eras; the prophets operate within covenant history yet point forward to the final reckoning.

Importantly, each message also contains a remnant promise, revealing wrath as ultimately restorative for the faithful. Such duality undermines both despair and complacency, compelling repentance while sustaining hope. Reading these texts today forces us to confront systemic injustices we have normalized.

1.1.4 New-Testament Fire: John 3:36 and Revelation's Bowls

Jesus' conversation with Nicodemus includes an often-ignored conclusion: "Whoever rejects the Son...God's wrath remains on him" (John 3:36). Far from softening the theme, the apostolic witness intensifies it; Paul warns that wrath is "being revealed" even now against ungodliness (Rom 1:18). The Apocalypse culminates this trajectory, describing bowls of wrath poured full strength (Rev 16:1). Yet Revelation frames these judgments as responses to martyr blood and unrepentant blasphemy, emphasizing justice rather than divine temper. The sustained symbolism—hail mixed with fire, scorched seas, poisoned rivers—underscores holistic impact: creation itself participates in the moral rectification. The cross-resurrection event anchors believers' confidence that wrath scheduled for the world has been vicariously borne, but the text will not allow us to trivialize future accountability. The New Testament, therefore, secures continuity with Sinai while amplifying both mercy and severity.

1.2 Why Wrath Is a Necessary Attribute

1.2.1 Moral Coherence in the Kingdom of Light

If God were indifferent to evil, the moral fabric of reality would unravel into cosmic absurdity. Wrath preserves coherence by declaring that every act of cruelty or deceit matters eternally. This attribute is therefore not secondary but essential to divine holiness, the antithesis of moral nihilism. Without wrath, justice would be reduced to human negotiation, vulnerable to power imbalances and cultural whims. Scripture presents the throne of God as established on righteousness and justice (Ps 97:2); wrath is the kinetic expression of that foundation when violated. Even unbelievers intuitively appeal to transcendent standards when confronted with atrocity, inadvertently acknowledging the necessity of ultimate retribution. Thus wrath secures the moral confidence that love itself requires, for love that never protects or avenges is sentimental pretense. In the kingdom of light, wrath and love are two rays from the same sun, illuminating and warming yet capable of burning.

1.2.2 Love's Protective Fury Against Evil

Parents who truly love their children cannot remain passive if a predator approaches; fierce intervention proves affection. Likewise, divine wrath is the protective side of love, acting against forces that wound and enslave His image-bearers. Exodus 22:22-24 warns that God will erupt in anger if widows and orphans are oppressed, linking wrath directly to compassion for the vulnerable. Christ's cleansing of the temple, with overturned tables and braided whip, embodies love defending worshipers from exploitation (John 2:13-17). These narratives correct the caricature that love and anger cannot coexist by showing that love often necessitates anger. The cross stands as the ultimate display, where the Son absorbs the Father's fury precisely because the Father loves the world (John 3:16). In that sense, wrath becomes the servant of redemption, clearing the path for reconciled relationship. To deny wrath is therefore to diminish divine love.

1.2.3 Judicial Integrity and Cosmic Order

Human courts demonstrate that impartiality demands proportionate sentencing; a judge who always pardons would be corrupt. God's wrath manifests His impeccably fair jurisprudence, guaranteeing that wrongs are neither ignored nor punished excessively. Romans 2:5 asserts that stubborn impenitence is "storing up wrath" for a day when righteous judgment will be revealed. This storage metaphor implies meticulous record-keeping rather than impulsive outburst, reinforcing integrity. Cosmic order depends on such reliability; planets obey gravitational laws because the Creator is consistent, and moral law shares that stability. The Psalms celebrate this reliability, proclaiming that truth and faithfulness surround Him (Ps 89:14). Thus wrath reinforces the universe's dependable structure: every action has meaningful consequence. When skeptics object to hell as disproportional, they often underestimate both the offense of sin against infinity and the majesty of offended holiness.

1.2.4 The Cross as Proof of Non-Negotiable Justice

Calvary exposes sin's gravity by necessitating a sacrifice of infinite worth; if God could relax justice, Christ need not die. Isaiah 53:10 says it pleased the Lord to crush the Servant, language that shocks until understood as judicial satisfaction. Paul explains that God set forth Jesus "to demonstrate His righteousness" so He could remain just while justifying the ungodly (Rom 3:25-26). The blood-soaked wood thus becomes the pulpit where wrath and mercy preach simultaneously. Every nail proclaims that law cannot be annulled; every cry of dereliction testifies that grace costs. Far from contradicting love, wrath magnifies it: only a God who hates sin enough to judge it can love sinners enough to rescue them. The cross therefore anchors both pastoral comfort and ethical seriousness, preventing cheap forgiveness. Any gospel that ignores wrath empties Calvary of necessity.

1.3 Misconceptions About an "Angry God"

1.3.1 Pagan Thunderers vs. Covenant Lord

Ancient deities such as Zeus hurled lightning bolts capriciously, reflecting human passions writ large. Critics often project that image onto the biblical God, conflating pagan myth with covenant revelation. Yet Scripture presents wrath as covenantal, tethered to promises and warnings delivered in advance. Deuteronomy 28 outlines blessings and curses, displaying predictability rather than volatility. Moreover, God's anger is never erotic or competitive; He has no rivals to threaten His self-esteem. Holiness, not ego, fuels His indignation. Comparing Yahweh to pagan storm-gods thus obscures the moral content of His wrath. Recognizing this distinction protects believers from shrinking back in servile fright and invites them instead to covenant loyalty.

1.3.2 Deistic Chill: Wrathless Moralism

Enlightenment thinkers stripped God of passion to secure philosophical respectability, but a distant clockmaker cannot inspire either fear or worship. This deistic chill persists in modern liberal theology, which treats divine anger as an embarrassing relic. The result is moralism without metaphysical teeth: exhortations to justice unmoored from punitive certainty. Micah's plea to "act justly" (Mic 6:8) gains weight because the same prophet announces wrath on those who oppress. Removing wrath thus undermines ethical urgency and fosters secular cynicism about religious relevance. Furthermore, a non-intervening deity leaves victims of atrocity without hope of vindication, effectively siding with oppressors. Authentic biblical faith refuses such sanitized transcendence, insisting that love and outrage coexist in perfect harmony.

1.3.3 Pop-Culture Caricatures and Satire

From internet memes to late-night monologues, the "angry sky-fairy" trope ridicules belief in divine judgment as primitive fearmongering. These caricatures ignore theological nuance and often rely on selective proof-texts while omitting passages that reveal patience and compassion. Satire can expose hypocrisy but can also harden ironic detachment, shielding the conscience from conviction. Proverbs 14:9 observes that fools mock at guilt, highlighting laughter as a common defense mechanism. Engaging such caricatures requires intellectual honesty and pastoral tenderness: believers must demonstrate that wrath is not a stand-alone obsession but integrated into a grand redemptive story. By contrasting superficial mockery with the cross's depth, Christians can invite skeptics to reconsider. Ultimately, caricatures collapse under the weight of real evil demanding response—genocide, trafficking, abuse—that jokes cannot erase.

1.3.4 Therapeutic Spirituality That Erases Judgment

Modern spirituality emphasizes self-esteem and emotional wellness, reshaping God into a cosmic life-coach. Such a therapeutic focus often reframes sin as dysfunction and wrath as negative energy, thereby neutralizing moral agency. Yet Jesus warns that hell is a place "where the worm does not die" (Mark 9:48), language too vivid to be metaphor for mild discomfort. Pastoral counseling that omits this dimension risks producing comfort without conversion, leaving souls at ease on the brink of ruin. Hebrews 10:26-27 cautions that deliberate sin after receiving knowledge of truth brings certain judgment, not mindfulness exercises. True healing involves diagnosis and radical cure, and wrath provides the diagnostic clarity that leads to the Great Physician. Ignoring wrath may soothe symptoms but leaves the underlying infection fatal.

1.4 Historical Theology: Voices Through the Centuries

1.4.1 Early Church Fathers on Divine Vengeance

Justin Martyr argued that the persecution of believers would be requited in God's time, anchoring hope in forthcoming judgment. Tertullian's *Apology* delights in the thought of imperial tyrants trembling, yet he frames this vindication within Christ's command to love enemies, creating a tension that refines rather than denies desire for justice. These writings illustrate that belief in wrath sustained martyr endurance; they were confident that Rome's lions would not roar the final word. The Fathers also guarded orthodoxy by warning that heresy incurred eschatological penalty, demonstrating wrath's role in doctrinal purity. Importantly, they linked punishment to moral restoration, anticipating purgation or corrective fire. Such nuances reveal early attempts to articulate wrath without compromising love. Through their witness, contemporary Christians inherit a legacy that treats wrath as pastoral resource, not embarrassment.

1.4.2 Medieval Allegory and Infernal Imagery

Dante's *Inferno* color-codes sins and matches contrapasso punishments, reflecting scholastic attempts to systematize justice. While some details owe more to imagination than exegesis, the enduring power of the poem lies in its moral clarity: choices shape destiny. Medieval sermons employed graphic depictions to awaken nominal Christians lulled by ritual familiarity. Stained-glass windows showed demons hauling souls to torment, a visual catechism for the illiterate. Critics dismiss this era as fear-mongering, yet it underscored seriousness amid plague and political upheaval. Wrath imagery gave suffering context and called sovereigns to account when earthly courts failed. Though allegorical excess warrants critique, the period illustrates how art and theology united to keep eternity before the mind.

1.4.3 Reformation Emphasis on Law and Gospel

Martin Luther's existential crisis stemmed from awareness of divine wrath, driving him to discover justification by faith. His breakthrough did not cancel wrath but located shelter in Christ, distinguishing law (which kills) from gospel (which makes alive). John Calvin likewise spoke of God's "terrible majesty," yet he found comfort in the same glory once mediated by the Mediator. The Reformers accused medieval piety of masking wrath with indulgences, insisting instead on imputed righteousness. Their preaching shook Europe because it wed unflinching condemnation with unmerited grace: wrath revealed the magnitude of salvation. Modern Protestantism inherits this dialectic but often truncates it, clinging to grace while muting the law. Revisiting Reformation homiletics can restore balance.

1.4.4 Edwards, Whitefield, and the Great Awakening Tone

Jonathan Edwards meticulously argued that sinners hang over hell by a slender thread sustained only by God's mercy, employing imagery like a spider dangling above fire. His purpose was not voyeuristic delight but urgent persuasion. George Whitefield's booming voice carried across open fields, and his tears testified that warnings flowed from compassion. Together they catalyzed social transformation, spurring philanthropy and abolitionist sentiment, demonstrating that wrath preaching can yield tangible mercy deeds. Critics later branded the movement emotionalism, yet careful reading of sermons reveals rigorous exegesis beneath pathos. The Awakening underscores that cultural renewal often begins with trembling hearts. Today's churches seeking revival might rediscover the synergy between doctrinal depth and rhetorical urgency.

1.5 Apocalyptic Imagery and Prophetic Warnings

1.5.1 Day-of-the-Lord Motifs in the Minor Prophets

Joel foretells a day of darkness when armies like locusts devour, yet he immediately issues a call to rend hearts, not garments (Joel 2:1-13). Amos warns complacent Samaria of an inescapable day when light turns to darkness (Am 5:18-20), exposing the folly of longing for judgment while living unjustly. These motifs present wrath as imminent yet conditional; repentance can shift outcome. They also universalize scope: the "day" concerns nations, not only Israel. By embedding cosmic upheaval in agrarian metaphors—withered vines, blood-red moon—prophets translate theological crisis into sensory experience. Thus apocalyptic language is sacramental, making invisible realities tangible. Modern readers often sensationalize or dismiss such imagery; a wiser approach hears it as ethical summons.

1.5.2 Cosmic Unraveling in Intertestamental Literature

Texts like 1 Enoch and 2 Baruch expand biblical visions of cataclysm, portraying stars falling and time itself collapsing. Though not canonical, these writings shaped first-century expectation and illuminate New Testament allusions. Their vivid hyperbole underscores that wrath is not mere personal experience but universe-wide reorientation. They assure persecuted minorities that emperors rule on borrowed time. The literature also introduces the notion of predetermined epochs, hinting at eschatological timetable later echoed in Revelation. While Christians need not accord these books scriptural authority, understanding them clarifies the cultural backdrop of Jesus' apocalypse discourse. The common thread is that judgment is both terrifying and hope-filled: it dethrones tyrants and enthrones righteousness.

1.5.3 Christ's Olivet Discourse and Wrath Deferred

In Matthew 24, Jesus predicts temple destruction, wars, and cosmic signs, but identifies the gospel's worldwide proclamation as prerequisite to the end. This sequence reveals wrath unfolding through historical convulsions rather than sudden annihilation. Luke's variant highlights mercy, urging disciples to flee Jerusalem, demonstrating wrath tempered by warning. The discourse balances urgency with delay: expect tribulation, yet no one knows the final hour. This tension discourages date-setting and fosters watchful obedience. Jesus situates wrath within covenant infidelity— Jerusalem's fall confirms prophetic consistency. Yet He also promises eventual gathering of the elect, fusing judgment and deliverance in one vision.

1.5.4 Revelation's Final Conflagration and Lake of Fire

John's apocalypse climaxes with Satan, death, and hades thrown into the lake of fire—a second death (Rev 20:14-15). Here wrath serves ultimate purification, eradicating evil's source. The lake is prepared for the devil, yet unrepentant humanity aligns with him, illustrating wrath as relational consequence. The preceding plague cycles display incremental judgments designed to provoke repentance (Rev 9:20-21), highlighting divine pedagogy. New Jerusalem's descent follows immediately, showing that wrath clears ground for new creation. Thus Revelation is not doom fixation but hope that evil's reign will end. Its imagery should ignite missionary urgency, for names not found in the Book of Life face eternal exclusion.

1.6 Wrath and Mercy in Christ's Teaching

1.6.1 "Woe" Sayings as Loving Alarm

Jesus pronounces woes on Chorazin and Bethsaida for spurning miracles more luminous than those given Tyre (Matt 11:21-24). These pronouncements arise from grief, not glee; Luke records Jesus weeping over Jerusalem's doom (Luke 19:41-44). The juxtaposition of lament and denunciation reveals wrath as compassionate protest. "Woe" in Hebrew tradition functions like a funeral dirge, implying that judgment is as much tragedy as penalty. The Savior thus warns as a physician reveals terminal prognosis, hoping diagnosis inspires treatment. Listeners are invited to consider severity in light of divine longing, not mere enforcement. This dynamic dismantles stereotypes that paint Christ gentle and the Father severe, for the Son embodies both kindness and sternness.

1.6.2 Parables of Separation: Wheat-and-Tares, Net Full of Fish

Parables employ familiar agrarian and maritime scenes to portray eschatological sorting. In Matthew 13, tares grow among wheat until harvest when reapers burn the weeds. The narrative affirms patience—premature rooting would harm wheat—yet assures eventual purge. Likewise, the dragnet gathers fish of every kind; worthless ones are cast away (Matt 13:47-50). Jesus explains plainly: "So it will be at the end of the age...angels will throw them into the blazing furnace." Parabolic technique disarms listeners with story before confronting them with choice. Separation underscores personal responsibility, countering universalist illusions. The emphasis on angelic agency indicates transcendence; judgment is not decided by earthly courts susceptible to error.

1.6.3 Gethsemane's Cup of Indignation

In the garden, Jesus speaks of a cup He must drink—a metaphor drawn from prophetic imagery of wrath (Isa 51:17; Jer 25:15). The anguish expressed—sweat like blood (Luke

22:44)—reveals that the agony of crucifixion is as much spiritual as physical. He faces abandonment under curse (Gal 3:13), entering darkness so believers may walk in light. The Father's willingness to let the Son drain this cup proves that wrath is neither illusion nor overstatement. It also demonstrates divine unity; the plan originates in eternal love, yet involves real penalty. Gethsemane invites worshipful silence rather than speculative analysis, for here mystery eclipses comprehension. The scene instructs that substitution is costlier than moral exhortation, underscoring gospel exclusivity.

1.6.4 Calvary: Wrath Absorbed, Grace Released

At noon the sky darkens, echoing plague of Egypt, signaling judgment (Matt 27:45). Jesus' cry "My God, my God, why have you forsaken me?" (Matt 27:46) quotes Psalm 22, integrating lament into passion. The tearing of the temple veil declares mission accomplished: access opens because wrath exhausted. Paul later celebrates that Christ disarmed rulers, triumphing over them on the cross (Col 2:15), showing wrath's cosmic effect. The event is both historical pivot and ontological upheaval: righteousness is revealed apart from law yet upholding law. Grace flows like living water because wrath fell like torrential hail. Every communion celebration re-enacts this exchange, keeping the church under the shadow of a satisfied sword.

1.7 Psychological and Cultural Dimensions

1.7.1 The Conscience as Echo of Judgment

Romans 2:15 describes Gentiles' consciences alternately accusing and excusing, testifying that moral awareness is universal. Even when suppressed, guilt resurfaces in anxiety, dreams, or social activism that seeks atonement through causes. Modern psychology labels guilt toxic when unresolved, but Scripture presents conviction as gift leading to repentance. The persistence of shame in ostensibly liberated cultures hints at an ineradicable moral imprint. Attempts to silence conscience through relativism often intensify neurosis, because the heart knows deeper law. Recognizing conscience as echo of wrath reframes inner disquiet as invitation, not mere pathology. Therapeutic interventions that respect this spiritual dimension can steer clients toward transformative grace.

1.7.2 Societal Rage and the Shadow of Divine Anger

Collective anger often mirrors suppressed awareness of injustice; riots, protest art, and cancel culture reflect yearning for judgment. When divine wrath is marginalized, societies attempt to enact ultimate justice through imperfect means, leading to cycles of retribution. René Girard's scapegoat theory suggests cultures defuse tension by blaming outsiders, yet the cross reveals and condemns this mechanism. Recognizing God's prerogative to judge can release communities from vengeful spirals, fostering forgiveness. Conversely, denying wrath perpetuates unending grievance. Thus theology shapes social dynamics, not merely private piety. Preaching divine judgment can, paradoxically, promote civic peace by relocating vengeance to God (Rom 12:19).

1.7.3 Modern Secular Anxiety and Forgotten Eschatology

Despite technological advancement, anxiety disorders proliferate, signaling existential dread. Secular narratives promise progress yet deliver fragile identities prone to collapse under failure or mortality reminders. Ecclesiastes observes that God has set eternity in human hearts (Eccl 3:11); suppressing eschatology leaves a vacuum filled by fear. Cultural fascination with apocalypse in films and games suggests sublimated awareness of wrath. These portrayals often exclude divine agency, presenting survivalism as salvation, yet the emotional undertow remains. Reintroducing biblical eschatology can convert aimless dread into purposeful hope anchored in Christ's return. Churches must address anxiety not only therapeutically but eschatologically.

1.7.4 Artistic Depictions From Dante to Dostoevsky

Great literature grapples with wrath's implications: Dante maps hell with poetic logic; Dostoevsky's *Brothers Karamazov* wrestles with divine justice amid suffering. Visual art—from Michelangelo's *Last Judgment* to contemporary installations—externalizes interior tremor. These works invite contemplation, provoking questions that dogma alone may not stir. They also risk sensationalism, yet their enduring appeal confirms human fascination with judgment themes. Engaging art theologically helps believers discern cultural longings that can be redirected to gospel answers. Artistic imagination complements expository preaching, offering metaphor where prose falters. Thus wrath fuels creativity even as it humbles pretension.

1.8 The Redemptive Purpose Behind Wrath

1.8.1 Awakening the Sleepers: Conviction's First Spark

Ephesians 5:14 calls the sleeper to rise, and historically awakenings begin not with comfort but alarm. Wrath serves as alarm clock, rousing souls anesthetized by culture. The prodigal son's famine was a form of temporal judgment that aroused memory of the father's house (Luke 15:14-17). Likewise, crisis often cracks self-reliance, making space for grace. Theological anthropology affirms that depravity dulls perception; wrath shocks the senses. Therefore preaching that omits warning may prolong slumber. Conviction is painful yet precursory to joy.

1.8.2 Restraining Common Grace in a Fallen World

Romans 1 portrays divine wrath revealed in handing people over to desires, highlighting passive judgment that lets sin reap its consequences. This restraint removal exposes evil's hideousness, deterring others and provoking repentance. Civil authorities, as ministers of wrath (Rom 13:4), restrain chaos, illustrating societal grace. Even natural disasters can function as memento mori, reminding humanity of creaturely dependence. Such temporal judgments are mercifully limited, intending to avert eternal loss. Acknowledging this framework prevents despair when calamities strike and fuels intercessory urgency.

1.8.3 Vindicating the Oppressed and Marginalized

Revelation's martyrs cry, "How long...until you judge?" (Rev 6:10), showing that wrath answers injustice. The Exodus narrative elevates this theme: God hears Israel's groans and responds with plagues that dismantle oppressive economies. Liberation theology sometimes reduces these acts to political upheaval, but Scripture frames them theologically as vindication emanating from covenant fidelity. Believers facing persecution today draw strength from knowing their tears are stored in God's bottle (Ps 56:8); wrath guarantees they are not forgotten. Such hope fortifies non-violent resistance and protects against bitterness. It also indicts privileged churches that ignore systemic sin, reminding them that wrath is impartial.

1.8.4 Catalyzing Worship That Is Both Trembling and Joyful

Psalm 2 commands rulers to "serve the Lord with fear and rejoice with trembling," fusing apparently contradictory emotions. Awareness of wrath deepens gratitude; the greater the peril, the sweeter the rescue. Early liturgies placed confession and Kyrie eleison before Eucharist, narrating movement from guilt to grace. Contemporary worship that skips lament and confession risks superficial celebration. Hebrews 12:28 urges worship with reverence because "our God is a consuming fire," situating New-Covenant praise within Sinai continuity. Thus wrath is not silenced by grace but absorbed into richer doxology.

1.9 Pastoral and Homiletical Applications

1.9.1 Preaching the Whole Counsel Without Relish or Evasion

Paul declared himself innocent of blood because he did not shrink from declaring all God's counsel (Acts 20:26-27). Preachers must resist two equal and opposite errors: sadistic delight in judgment or cowardly avoidance. Faithful exposition lets the text set tone, trusting the Spirit to apply. Illustrations should serve clarity, not entertainment. Balance is achieved by coupling warnings with invitations, mirroring biblical rhythm. Humility compels the preacher to remember personal need of mercy while addressing others. Prayer saturates preparation, seeking broken heart rather than theatrical performance.

1.9.2 Counseling Souls Haunted by Guilt or Numbed by Sin

Pastoral care encounters two extremes: the trembling penitent who doubts pardon and the complacent churchgoer unfazed by rebellion. For the former, the remedy is magnifying the sufficiency of atonement, showing that wrath satisfied cannot resurface. For the latter, counselors may gently expose consequences scripture delineates, praying conviction pierces armor of religiosity. Both require patient listening and targeted scripture. James 5:16 connects confession with healing, underscoring community role. Counselors who grasp wrath and grace wield sharper diagnostic tools, distinguishing worldly sorrow from godly sorrow (2 Cor 7:10).

1.9.3 Corporate Liturgies Shaped by Gravity and Grace

Historic liturgies embed confession, assurance, and thanksgiving, mapping gospel narrative weekly. Including readings such as Romans 5:9-11 anchors assurance in objective work. Musical selections can alternate minor-key lament with triumphant hymns, mirroring cross and resurrection. Communion self-examination (1 Cor 11:28-29) prevents casual approach. Visual symbols—cross, baptismal font—remind worshipers of wrath quenched and life granted.

Such practices form disciples over time, combating consumerist worship models.

1.9.4 Evangelistic Appeals That Unite Terror and Tenderness

Peter's Pentecost sermon declared crucifixion guilt before offering repentance and baptism (Acts 2:36-38). Effective evangelism follows this pattern, clarifying peril to heighten appreciation for deliverance. Street preaching caricatures notwithstanding, most conversions occur through relationship where truth is spoken in love. Apologists can connect wrath to moral outrage about injustice, bridging cultural values to gospel truth. Testimonies of rescued addicts or former traffickers concretize sin's bondage and grace's power. Invitations must rely on Spirit conviction, avoiding manipulation. Joy in ambassador's heart authenticates message of reconciliation (2 Cor 5:20).

Conclusion

Divine wrath, far from being an embarrassing relic, is the molten core of biblical revelation, radiating moral coherence, protective love, and judicial integrity. Its flames illuminate the cross, the prophets, the conscience, and the liturgy, ensuring that neither sin nor suffering slides into cosmic insignificance. When rightly understood, it humbles the arrogant, vindicates the oppressed, and propels the rescued into songs of astonished gratitude. A church that forgets wrath forfeits urgency; a culture that mocks it cultivates despair. Yet for those who heed the warning, wrath becomes the dark canvas on which the colors of grace gleam with unmatched brilliance. May the terrible majesty explored in these pages drive each reader not to hopeless dread but to steadfast refuge in the One who drank the cup to its dregs so enemies might become beloved children.

Chapter 2. Human Frailty Suspended Over the Abyss

A trembling hush often settles over the soul when it pauses long enough to consider how precariously it occupies a place between birth and eternity. The previous chapter meditated on the blazing holiness that energizes divine wrath; this chapter turns the lens upon humanity itself—creatures of breath and bone whose every heartbeat is a fragile mercy. To explore human frailty is neither morbid fascination nor sentimental melancholy. It is an exercise in intellectual honesty and spiritual wisdom, for Scripture insists that those who learn to number their days gain a heart of wisdom (Psalm 90 :12). We will observe how biblical narratives, philosophical reflections, and contemporary anxieties converge to expose the myth of self-security. Along the way, we will see that mortality, when faced squarely, becomes a gracious tutor, steering sinners away from presumption and toward the refuge of Christ. Only within such sober awareness can an authentic longing for grace ignite. With that aim, we now descend into the manifold lessons of human fragility.

Prelude - A Fragile Thread Between Time and Eternity

The heartbeat as heaven-timed metronome

Every pulse that reverberates through the arteries is a silent decree from the throne of God, because in Him "we live and move and have our being" (Acts 17 :28). Medical science can describe electrical impulses that trigger ventricular contractions, yet it cannot supply the metaphysical reason that one more beat occurs rather than none. If God were to withdraw His sustaining word for a single instant, the heart would cease mid-systole, and with it every cherished ambition. This regular thump—so easily taken for granted—functions as a holy metronome that should keep our days in humble rhythm, reminding us that we are "a mist that appears for a little time and then vanishes" (James 4 :14). Ironically, people often notice their heartbeat only when it races in fear or falters in illness, as though fragility must shout before it is heeded. The psalmist's assertion that "my times are in Your hand" (Psalm 31 :15) renders each heartbeat a divine signature rather than a mechanical reflex. To feel the pulse, therefore, is to touch a sacrament of dependency. Recognizing this dependency dismantles the illusion of autonomous existence and prepares the mind to consider eternity.

How plagues, wars, and accidents expose our contingency

Cataclysmic events punctuate history like divine parentheses, interrupting complacent narratives of progress and control. The Black Death of the fourteenth century cut down one-third of Europe, reminding castles and cottages alike that flesh is dust. World wars in the twentieth century leveled cities and shattered technological optimism, showing how swiftly human ingenuity can turn on itself. In more recent memory, a microscopic virus spread across the globe in months, humbling economic superpowers and stalling aircraft fleets that once stitched continents together in hours. Even mundane accidents—a texting driver, a falling tree limb, an aneurysm rupturing without warning—prove that danger need not wear apocalyptic costume to accomplish its task. Scripture is unembarrassed by this reality: Jesus cites a collapsing tower that killed eighteen people in Siloam as evidence of universal vulnerability (Luke 13 :4-5). Such events interrogate the myth that wealth, education, or geopolitics can shield a soul from the abyss. Each calamity is, paradoxically, a mercy, jolting humanity awake to the brevity of life.

The spiritual usefulness of memento mori disciplines

Early Christian monks kept skulls on their desks and inscribed phrases such as *hora fugit, memento mori*—"the hour flies, remember death." Far from cultivating morbid despair, the practice sharpened gratitude and vigilance. The Bible itself recommends a similar posture, declaring that "it is better to go to the house of mourning than the house of feasting" because grief teaches wisdom (Ecclesiastes 7 :2-4). Modern believers can recover these disciplines through periodic silence, cemetery walks, or Ash-Wednesday liturgies that trace crosses of dust upon foreheads. Digital calendars could place a daily notification—*You are dust, and to dust you shall return* (Genesis 3 :19)—beside meetings and meal-prep schedules, baptizing time management in eternal perspective. Such practices are not gloomy fixations but luminous reminders that life's value rises precisely because it is fleeting. They strip away trivial preoccupations, making room for repentance and generosity. Most importantly, *memento mori* aims the heart toward Christ, who alone can escort mortals through the valley of the shadow of death.

2.1 The Ephemeral Breath of Existence

2.1.1 Dust to Dust: The Genesis Frame

The opening chapters of Genesis establish anthropology upon a profound tension: humanity is both sculpted from dirt and animated by the very breath of God (Genesis 2 :7). That duality means dignity cohabits with fragility; nobility cannot evade vulnerability. When Adam and Eve rebel, the divine verdict—"for you are dust, and to dust you shall return"

(Genesis 3 :19)—reasserts creatureliness under the specter of death. This pronouncement was not merely punitive but revelatory, exposing what sin obscured: independence is an illusion. Across millennia, funerals repeat the words "earth to earth, ashes to ashes, dust to dust," grounding grief in the biblical storyline. Soil thrown upon a coffin is therefore a testimony to both origin and destiny apart from redemption. Recognizing dusty beginnings curbs the pride that boasts of achievements as self-generated. It also accelerates the quest for a second breath—the Spirit's regeneration (John 3 :5-8)—that alone conquers mortality. Genesis thus frames human life as a brief arc whose beginning and end meet in the same handful of clay unless grace intervenes.

2.1.2 Vapor, Shadow, Grass: Poetic Images in Psalms & Wisdom

Hebrew poetry excels at compressing oceans of meaning into terse metaphor. The psalmist confesses, "Indeed, every man at his best state is altogether vapor" (Psalm 39 :5 NKJV), and again, "As for man, his days are like grass ... the wind passes over it, and it is gone" (Psalm 103 :15-16). Ecclesiastes repeats the refrain "vanity of vanities," with *hebel* denoting breath that dissipates on a cold morning (Ecclesiastes 1 :2). Shadows lengthening across evening walls symbolize ambition fading before dusk. These images do more than evoke fragility; they critique idolatry of permanence. To invest ultimate meaning in vapor is the height of folly, yet industries of branding, architecture, and social media thirst for lasting legacy. The wisdom literature invites a healthier ambition—to fear the LORD, which "prolongs life" in a qualitative sense (Proverbs 10 :27). By internalizing these metaphors, believers learn to hold possessions loosely and relationships tenderly, knowing both may vanish with sunrise.

2.1.3 Statistical Odds of Survival: Modern Mortality Data

Actuarial tables translate poetic brevity into cold numbers, revealing the probability of death by age, geography, and lifestyle. While life expectancy in many countries hovers beyond seventy-five, the distribution curve hides individual stories of neonatal loss and youthful accidents. Cardiovascular disease claims one-third of global deaths, cancers another sixth, and yet few people schedule daily life around those odds. Insurance companies price premiums to account for risk, but souls seldom calculate eternity with equal diligence. Jesus challenges such statistics when He asks, "Which of you by being anxious can add a single hour to his span of life?" (Matthew 6 :27 ESV). Modern data, rather than granting control, emphasizes unpredictability; a gym membership lowers risk but does not nullify it. Therefore, statistical knowledge ought to prompt spiritual preparedness, not complacent odds-gaming. If anything, numbers confirm ancient metaphors—life's candle flickers even in sanitized hospital rooms equipped with cutting-edge devices.

2.1.4 Life Expectancy and the Illusion of Control

Technological societies often treat life expectancy like a contract: follow health guidelines, and additional decades are guaranteed. This mindset surfaces in marketing—the right supplement promises "cellular longevity," the latest smartwatch monitors arrhythmias in real time. While stewardship of the body is biblical (1 Corinthians 6 :19-20), presumption is not; the rich fool in Jesus' parable strategizes bigger barns for longer enjoyment, only to hear, "Fool! This night your soul is required of you" (Luke 12 :20). Control is further shattered by congenital disease, genetic lottery, or sudden catastrophe. In the Bible, even King Hezekiah's fifteen-year extension after earnest prayer (Isaiah 38 :5) underscores sovereignty rather than formula. When believers treat health as conditional immortality, disappointment can mutate into anger at God, revealing idolatry. A wiser posture thanks Him for daily bread while acknowledging that tomorrow may not dawn. True security flows not from extended chronology but from eternal life, which transcends calendars altogether (John 11 :25-26).

2.2 The Illusion of Self-Security

2.2.1 Economic Prosperity as False Fortress

Wealth often masquerades as a citadel against contingency, yet Proverbs warns, "The wealth of the rich is their fortified city; they imagine it a wall too high to scale" (Proverbs 18 :11 NIV). Market crashes, hyperinflation, or medical bills can crumble fortunes overnight, revealing that imagined bastions were built of paper. Jesus' encounter with the rich young ruler (Mark 10 :17-27) illustrates how possessions entangle the will, making surrender seem impossible. In modern terms, diversified portfolios and real-estate holdings cannot purchase one minute's reprieve from death. Ecclesiastes notes that riches sometimes keep their owners from sleep because anxiety about loss surges with accumulation (Ecclesiastes 5 :12). The gospel counters by storing treasure in heaven, "where moth and rust do not destroy" (Matthew 6 :19-20). Recognizing the transience of money enables generosity, which ironically converts temporal assets into eternal dividends. Economic prosperity becomes a tool rather than a trap only when relinquished to God's purposes.

2.2.2 Technological Hubris and the Myth of Mastery

From Babel's bricks to Silicon Valley's algorithms, humanity has sought to engineer permanence. Smart homes, autonomous vehicles, and CRISPR gene edits promise to extend life and eradicate disease, yet each innovation introduces new vulnerabilities—cyberattacks, ethical dilemmas, unforeseen side effects. The Titanic was advertised as unsinkable; within days it lay on an icy ocean floor, a steel parable against hubris. God's rhetorical question to Job—"Can you bind the chains of the Pleiades?" (Job 38 :31)—still silences technophilic boasting. While Christians applaud science as exploration of divine order, they resist equating knowledge with sovereignty. The Lord scattered Babel precisely because unbounded collaboration in pride would multiply evil (Genesis 11 :6-9). Thus every server outage or software glitch should remind users that binary code cannot mend fallen nature. Dependence on technology without repentance before its Creator only deepens alienation.

2.2.3 Health Idolatry and Biohacking Dreams

Gyms glow around the clock, supplement stores burst with antioxidants, and wearable trackers gamify sleep cycles, collectively forming a quasi-religion of bodily optimization. While stewardship is commendable, obsession betrays fear of the abyss. The Apostle Paul affirms bodily discipline but notes that "godliness is of value in every way, as it holds promise for the present life and also for the life to come" (1 Timothy 4 :8). Biohacking prophets envision uploading consciousness to cloud servers, echoing Gnostic fantasies of escaping flesh— yet Scripture heralds a bodily resurrection, not a digital afterlife (1 Corinthians 15 :42-44). Ironically, hyper-focus on longevity can diminish life's richness, reducing meals to macros and friendships to performance metrics. Health becomes a fickle deity demanding endless sacrifice without offering real security. True wholeness arises when bodies are presented as living sacrifices (Romans 12 :1), resting in the promise of glorification rather than hacking decay.

2.2.4 Insurance, Investments, and the Uninsured Soul

Policies safeguard homes from fire, cars from collision, and income from disability, yet no underwriter can insure against divine judgment. Jesus warns, "What will it profit a man if he gains the whole world and forfeits his soul?" (Matthew 16 :26). Eternal risk dwarfs temporal contingencies, but marketing rarely highlights this liability. Ironically, the meticulous planner who updates beneficiaries may neglect spiritual legacy, leaving heirs with wealth but no wisdom. Early Christians stored parchments of Scripture more zealously than deeds of land, convinced that the Word can "build you up and give you an inheritance" (Acts 20 :32). Modern believers might ask whether their estate plans include testimony of faith or merely asset distribution. Heavenly inheritance rests on adoption through Christ, not annuities. Thus, the only premium that secures the future has already been paid in blood; ignoring that payment leaves the account eternally overdue.

2.3 Gazing Into the Abyss—Defining Ultimate Loss

2.3.1 Hell as Relational Exile From God's Face

Many conceive of hell as fiery chamber, yet the most terrifying aspect is relational: eternal separation from the source of light, life, and joy (2 Thessalonians 1 :9). The Bible describes the lost as banished "from the presence of the Lord," echoing Cain's dread after murder (Genesis 4 :14). Because humanity was fashioned *for* communion, exile mutilates identity; the soul languishes like a branch severed from vine (John 15 :6). Physical metaphors—flame, darkness, worm—likely gesture toward realities too dreadful for literal depiction. The abyss yawns as a relational vacuum where every good gift is withdrawn, leaving only the desiccated husk of self-absorption. Recognizing hell as exile rather than divine tantrum underscores justice: those who spurn God receive the autonomy they demanded—forever. This view intensifies evangelistic urgency, for reconciliation, not merely rescue from pain, is the gospel's aim. Heaven's happiness is the unveiled face of God; hell's horror is that face hidden eternally.

2.3.2 Degrees of Consequence: Justice Fitted to Deeds

Jesus speaks of varying stripes administered to servants based on knowledge and action (Luke 12 :47-48), suggesting calibrated punishment. Revelation lists sins preventing entry into the city but notes that books were opened, "and the dead were judged ... according to what they had done" (Revelation 20 :12). Such passages refute caricatures of indiscriminate wrath; divine justice is exquisitely exact. The moral weight of an action correlates with creaturely capacity and received revelation. This precision magnifies the seriousness of every choice, for nothing slips through cosmic auditing. Civil courts approximate equity, but God's tribunal requires no forensic error margins. Believers therefore cultivate integrity in hidden motives, knowing that the Judge sifts heart and marrow (Hebrews 4 :12-13). For the unrepentant, the prospect of detailed reckoning intensifies dread—eternity will not be served a generic sentence but a personally fitted consequence.

2.3.3 Eternal-Conscious Torment Versus Annihilationist Hopes

Throughout church history, some have hoped that the wicked will simply cease to exist, citing phrases like "the soul that sins shall die" (Ezekiel 18 :4). Yet Jesus describes a fate where "their worm does not die and the fire is not quenched" (Mark 9 :48), indicating ongoing awareness. Revelation pictures smoke of torment ascending "forever and ever" (Revelation 14 :11). Annihilationism aims to safeguard God's goodness, yet it may undercut His justice by reducing sin's gravity. The cross's agony, intended to absorb eternal penalty, suggests equivalence in scale between offense and atonement; if punishment were momentary, substitution would be disproportionate. While orthodox believers debate details, all agree that ultimate loss is irreversible and dreadful. This doctrinal sobriety guards evangelism from casual invitations and discipleship from superficiality. Whatever form judgment takes, it eclipses every temporal sorrow, confirming Jesus' warning to fear Him who can destroy both soul and body in hell (Matthew 10 :28).

2.3.4 The Psychological Weight of Meaninglessness

Apart from hope of resurrection, mortality precipitates nihilism; Paul concedes, "If the dead are not raised, 'Let us eat and drink, for tomorrow we die'" (1 Corinthians 15 :32). Existential philosophers like Camus saw the absurdity of searching for meaning in a closed universe, likening life to Sisyphus pushing a stone uphill only for it to roll down again. Suicide rates often correlate with loss of purpose, demonstrating that psychological health feeds on transcendent significance. The abyss terrifies not only because of pain but because of purposeless continuation or obliteration. Christ's gospel alleviates this burden by joining suffering to future glory (Romans 8 :18). For the believer, labor is "not in vain in the Lord" (1 Corinthians 15 :58), reframing even mundane tasks. Thus, the antidote to existential despair is not distraction but resurrection hope rooted in historical reality. Failing to embrace that hope leaves the soul teetering over endless void.

2.4 Biblical Narratives That Expose Frailty

2.4.1 Babel's Collapse and the Shattered Tower

The tower-builders of Genesis 11 sought name and security, attempting to breach heaven with baked bricks. God's descent to scatter them reveals comedic disparity between human ambition and divine sovereignty. Their project crumbled not because of engineering flaws but because of spiritual hubris. The sudden confusion of language birthed cultural fragmentation that endures today, a perpetual reminder that unity without humility breeds ruin. Archaeology uncovers ziggurats eroded by time, mute monuments to thwarted aspirations. Babel teaches that globalized progress, devoid of reverence, is suspended over judgment. Modern skyscrapers etched against city skylines may similarly testify to techno-pride if unaccompanied by repentance. Thus the narrative punctures illusions of permanence and calls each generation to submit plans to the Architect whose blueprints span eternity.

2.4.2 Nebuchadnezzar's Madness and the Limits of Empire

Daniel 4 recounts an emperor strolling on his palace roof, boasting of "the great Babylon ... built by my mighty power." A heavenly voice decrees insanity; the king lives like an ox until he acknowledges "the Most High rules" (Daniel 4 :30-34). This story dramatizes neurological fragility: one synaptic malfunction can topple a throne. Empire builders today—corporate moguls, political leaders, cultural influencers—are one stroke, scandal, or market crash away from ruin. Nebuchadnezzar's restoration only after praising God illustrates that sanity itself is a gift, not an entitlement. The narrative urges rulers to steward power with trembling, for authority derives from heaven (John 19 :11). It also comforts marginalized believers by highlighting God's ability to humble oppressors overnight. Frailty, therefore, haunts palaces no less than hovels.

2.4.3 The Rich Fool's Midnight Summons (Luke 12)

Jesus presents a landowner whose bumper crop incites barn-building rather than benevolence. He speaks to his soul as though it were a storage unit: "Soul, you have ample goods laid up ... relax, eat, drink, be merry." That night, God demands his soul, calling him "fool." The parable juxtaposes agricultural blessing with spiritual bankruptcy, demonstrating that prosperity can actually accelerate peril when it fuels presumption. The timing—midnight—emphasizes unpredictability, while the divine address exposes accountability. This story unsettles hearers across socioeconomic strata; even modest savings accounts can nurture similar self-talk. Jesus concludes by urging riches toward God, directing hearts from barns toward kingdom philanthropy. Thus, the narrative unmasks the abyss hidden beneath apparent abundance.

2.4.4 Herod's Worm-Eaten Throne (Acts 12)

When Herod Agrippa I basks in sycophantic praise—"the voice of a god!"—an angel strikes him, and he is "eaten by worms and breathed his last." Luke juxtaposes royal pomp with biological decay, compressing the distance between throne and grave. This grisly exit echoes Isaiah's taunt over Babylon's fallen king: "maggots are spread under you" (Isaiah 14 :11). Historians suggest intestinal parasites slowly consumed Herod, a living metaphor of power corroded from within. The passage immediately notes, "But the word of God increased and multiplied," contrasting mortal authority with enduring gospel. Herod's fate warns modern celebrities and politicians that applause can mask rot; the abyss opens beneath unchecked vanity. For believers, the episode bolsters confidence that persecutors remain under God's scalpel.

2.5 Philosophical Echoes of Precarious Being

2.5.1 Existential Angst From Ecclesiastes to Camus

The Teacher in Ecclesiastes surveys accomplishments—wisdom, pleasure, toil—and pronounces them hebel, chasing wind. Centuries later, philosophers like Kierkegaard, Nietzsche, and Camus articulate dread and absurdity in a God-eclipsed cosmos. Each diagnosis acknowledges a rift between human longing for permanence and the world's transient fabric. Camus' parable of Sisyphus rolling a stone eternally resonates with cubicle workers repeating tasks that evaporate in quarterly reports. Yet Ecclesiastes hints at remedy: "Fear God and keep His commandments" (Ecclesiastes 12 :13). Existentialism without revelation ends in either revolt or resignation; the gospel offers redemption. Thus secular angst both critiques superficial religion and begs for transcendent resolution. The church can engage thinkers honestly, validating their questions while presenting Christ as the anchor that stabilizes meaning amid flux. Ignoring philosophy leaves many dangling without interpretive nets.

2.5.2 Pascal's Wager Revisited for a Skeptical Age

Blaise Pascal argued that rational self-interest favors wagering on God's existence, for eternal gain outweighs finite loss. Critics dismiss the wager as calculating, yet it underscores human uncertainty and risk. Modern risk-management theories echo Pascal: hedge funds diversify because ignorance of future events is certain. If the abyss is even a remote possibility, wisdom demands preparation. Hebrews 11 :6 asserts that God rewards those who seek Him, framing faith as informed trust. In a pluralistic era, Pascal's logic can initiate dialogue by moving debate from abstract proofs to pragmatic consequence. However, the gospel ultimately invites love, not mere probability calculus; the wager may open the door, but the cross compels the heart. Still, contemplating wagers reveals how many live as though odds of judgment were zero—an irrational gamble.

2.5.3 Stoic Memento Mori *and the Virtue of Acceptance*

Stoicism instructs disciples to rehearse death daily, cultivating serenity through acceptance of fate (*amor fati*). Marcus Aurelius, writing during plagues and wars, urged calm awareness that life is loaned. This resonates with Paul, who learned contentment regardless of circumstance (Philippians 4 :11-13), yet Christian hope exceeds Stoic resignation by anticipating resurrection. Where Stoicism steels the mind, the gospel softens the heart with relational promises. Still, Stoic practices—negative visualization, voluntary discomfort—can help believers detach from luxury's grip. James urges readers to say, "If the Lord wills, we will live and do this or that" (James 4 :15), blending humility with purpose. Thus, Stoic emphasis on mortality can serve as preparatory pedagogy, though it must be baptized into eschatological joy.

2.5.4 Secular Humanism's Hope and Its Hard Ceiling

Humanism extols human potential while acknowledging finitude; it invests in education, justice, and art, trusting progress to outpace peril. Yet without transcendence, its ceiling is the heat death of the universe—entropy extinguishing consciousness. Bertrand Russell conceded that "only on the firm foundation of unyielding despair" can humanity build meaning. Scripture offers starker honesty and brighter promise: the present creation will indeed dissolve, but a new heavens and earth await (2 Peter 3 :10-13). Humanism's ethic often mirrors biblical morality, borrowing dignity while denying its source. When confronted by pandemics or genocide, humanistic optimism strains. Christians can affirm common-grace achievements yet point beyond them to a kingdom "that cannot be shaken" (Hebrews 12 :28). Otherwise, noble endeavors hover over an abyss they cannot bridge.

2.6 Sin's Erosion of Human Stability

2.6.1 Addiction and the Hijacked Will

Sin warps freedom into bondage, as Jesus notes: "Everyone who sins is a slave to sin" (John 8 :34). Addiction, whether chemical or digital, demonstrates how desires override reason, enslaving the will. Neurological scans reveal dopamine loops that drown executive function, yet Scripture diagnosed this slavery millennia ago. The alcoholic who promises sobriety tomorrow but drinks tonight illustrates Paul's lament: "I do not do the good I want" (Romans 7 :19). Societal frailty increases as epidemics of opioids or pornography drain productivity and fracture families. Government programs target symptoms; the gospel addresses root cravings by offering superior pleasure in God (Psalm 16 :11). Addiction's grip exposes vulnerability: a brain chemical can topple resolve. Therefore, personal frailty is not merely physical but volitional, requiring supernatural liberation.

2.6.2 Violence as Accelerant of Societal Decay

From Cain's blood-spattered field to urban shootings, violence accelerates humanity's descent toward chaos. Genesis 6 :11 links pre-flood corruption to violence filling the earth. Swords and plowshares vie for prominence in every era; when swords win, cultures teeter over the abyss. War refugees, orphans, and PTSD survivors testify that one trigger pull reverberates across generations. Jesus' beatitude—"Blessed are the peacemakers" (Matthew 5 :9)—implies that peace-breaking is cursed, advancing entropy. Every homicide secretly preaches mortality, reminding survivors of their own breakable bodies. Christian witness, therefore, includes modeling non-retaliation and advocating justice that stems violence. Yet final peace awaits the Lamb who will end war (Revelation 21 :4), highlighting ongoing vulnerability until His return.

2.6.3 Idolatry and the Fragmented Self

Idols promise control—fertility, fame, fortune—while siphoning life. Habakkuk mocks idols that "have no breath" (Habakkuk 2 :19), inadvertently picturing idolaters as echoing their lifeless gods. Psychologically, worship of status or pleasure fractures identity, forcing the self into constant image-management. David's adultery spiraled into murder and public scandal, unraveling his household (2 Samuel 12 :10-14). Modern idolatry hides behind career ladders or influencer metrics but wields equal lethality. Fragmentation breeds anxiety, for the idol demands more while delivering less. Until allegiance is reoriented toward the triune God, who integrates desires, the self dangles in internal abyss. Repentance heals fragmentation, reassembling purpose under a singular love (Mark 12 :30).

2.6.4 Cultural Patterns of Dehumanization

Sin metastasizes from individual hearts into societal structures—slavery, racism, exploitation—turning image-bearers into commodities. Prophets decry those who "sell the righteous for silver and the needy for a pair of sandals" (Amos 2 :6). Dehumanization hollows out both victim and perpetrator, eroding communal resilience. Nazi ideology, rooted in pseudo-science, murdered millions and left Europe psychologically scarred. Contemporary forms include human trafficking and algorithmic bias, subtly assigning worth by profit margins. Such sin exposes collective frailty; a civilization can implode when empathy evaporates. The gospel restores dignity by announcing that Christ took on flesh, forever uniting God to humanity. Failure to honor this incarnation keeps societies flirting with the abyss of barbarism.

2.7 The Anatomy of Presumption

2.7.1 Cognitive Biases That Mask Mortality

Psychologists identify optimism bias—the tendency to believe bad things happen to others, not us. This bias helps soldiers charge battlefields, but it also helps teenagers speed through red lights. Scripture counters with sober realism: "You do not know what your life will be like tomorrow" (James 4 :14). Heavenly wisdom dismantles self-deception using law, prophecy, and parable. Disaster tends to appear sudden only to the unprepared; Noah spent decades building an ark in plain sight. Believers combat bias through disciplines of examination and confession, inviting the Spirit to expose hidden faults (Psalm 139 :23-24). Community accountability further punctures illusions, as friends admonish one another. Without such practices, cognitive biases escort souls toward cliffs disguised as level ground.

2.7.2 Religious Formalism as a Safety Blanket

Attending services, reciting creeds, and tithing can foster complacency if unaccompanied by heart renewal. Jeremiah warns Judah not to chant "the temple of the LORD" as talisman while committing injustice (Jeremiah 7 :4-11). Pharisees perfected ritual while plotting murder, proving that liturgy without love breeds presumption. Jesus likens such religiosity to whitewashed tombs—ornate but internally rotten (Matthew 23 :27). Modern parallels include nominal Christianity that checks moral boxes yet ignores the poor or tolerates hidden sin. Sacraments become fire insurance rather than fellowship. Genuine faith, by contrast, trembles at God's word and rejoices in gospel grace. Only the Spirit can convert routine into relational obedience, turning forms into channels of life.

2.7.3 Prosperity-Gospel Promises and Spiritual Myopia

Preachers who equate faith with financial success inadvertently build theology on shifting sand. When illness or bankruptcy strikes, adherents either blame themselves or indict God, revealing foundation cracks. Paul's catalog of sufferings—whippings, shipwrecks, hunger (2 Corinthians 11 :23-27)—refutes any guarantee of comfort. Yet prosperity messages flourish where materialism reigns, offering cosmic endorsement of consumer dreams. This myopia blinds hearers to eternal treasure, chaining their hopes to depreciating assets. Jesus warns Laodicea, "You say, I am rich ... not realizing you are wretched, pitiable, poor" (Revelation 3 :17). True wealth is friendship with God; losing it is abyss indeed. Thus, prosperity gospel functions as anesthetic that numbs frailty awareness until judgment awakens it abruptly.

2.7.4 Entertainment Culture and Eternal Amnesia

Screens saturate attention with ceaseless streams of trivia, sports, and dramas, drowning reflection. The prophet Amos condemns those who "sing idle songs ... but are not grieved over the ruin of Joseph" (Amos 6 :5-6). Constant amusement blunts conscience, leaving little space to ponder mortality. Neil Postman warned of "amusing ourselves to death," a phrase now even more pertinent amid algorithm-tailored feeds. Sabbath rhythms resist this tide, inviting silence where God's whisper can be heard. If entertainment remains unchecked, souls may reach eternity having never asked why they existed. The gospel invites joy, yet joy differs from distraction: it flows from truth embraced, not evaded. Therefore, Christians curate media with discernment, lest pixels pave a glittering road to oblivion.

2.8 Fragility in the Face of Cosmic Hazards

2.8.1 Pandemics and Microbial Threats

Invisible microbes humble superpowers: Yersinia pestis, influenza, HIV, SARS-CoV-2. Each pathogen sidesteps borders and armies, infiltrating lungs and bloodstreams. Levitical laws on quarantine (Leviticus 13) anticipated germ theory by millennia, reflecting divine care for communal health. Pandemics expose inequities, as the poor suffer higher mortality—reminding society of its interdependence. They also stir eschatological speculation, echoing apocalyptic pestilence imagery (Luke 21 :11). Medical advances mitigate but cannot eradicate outbreaks; antibiotic resistance looms as future crisis. Thus microbes preach: humanity rides a biological knife-edge. Believers respond with both compassion—healing ministries, vaccine advocacy—and lament, groaning for redemption of bodies (Romans 8 :23).

2.8.2 Climate Catastrophes and Natural Disasters

Hurricanes flatten coastlines, wildfires devour suburbs, earthquakes crumble infrastructure—all within hours. Creation groans under Adam's curse, subjected "to futility" (Romans 8 :20-22). While stewardship can reduce carbon footprints or improve building codes, ultimate control eludes experts. Job 38-41 depicts God commanding snow and lightning, reminding humans of elemental subservience. Disasters reveal both physical fragility and social fault lines, as marginalized communities quake under disproportionate losses. They invite corporate repentance for environmental negligence and idolatry of consumption. Though insurance may rebuild houses, only resurrection rebuilds hope. Christ's calming of the storm foreshadows a day when seas will be glass, not fury (Revelation 15 :2).

2.8.3 Nuclear Risk and Technological Backfire

The splitting of the atom unlocked energy that powers cities and threatens extinction. Cold-War doomsday clocks hovered seconds from midnight; rogue states and terrorist ambitions keep hands twitching near red buttons. This tension illustrates how dominion mandate skewed by sin weaponizes creation. Isaiah's prophecy of nations beating swords into plowshares (Isaiah 2 :4) mocks missile stockpiles. Cyber warfare adds complexity, as code can hijack reactors or grids. Such perils suspend humanity over self-inflicted abyss. Believers pray for leaders "that we may live peaceful and quiet lives" (1 Timothy 2 :2), yet trust not in diplomacy alone but in the Prince of Peace who will abolish war. Until then, nuclear shadows lengthen across fragile flesh.

2.8.4 Astrophysical Perils: Solar Flares and Meteors

Beyond terrestrial crises, cosmic threats lurk—solar flares frying power grids, asteroids crashing like the one that ended dinosaurs. NASA tracks Near-Earth Objects, acknowledging margins of error. Psalm 19 praises the sun's course but also implies dependency on God's regulation. Jesus declares celestial signs will precede His return (Luke 21 :25-26), suggesting that cosmic instability heralds eschatological climax. Humanity's inability to divert large asteroids underscores smallness within vast universe. Each shooting star should remind stargazers of potential impact sites. Yet Christians gaze heavens with hope, for from there the Savior will descend (Philippians 3 :20), converting peril into promise.

2.9 Toward a Wise Heart—Embracing Mortality

2.9.1 Numbering Our Days (Psalm 90)

Moses prays for wisdom to count days, contrasting divine eternity with human brevity. This arithmetic is not morose; it guides priorities. Setting life expectancy beside kingdom calling helps allocate gifts toward eternal yields. Service replaces hoarding when time feels short. Pilgrim metaphors— tents, journeys, exile—saturate Scripture, shaping disciples who travel light. Counting days also fuels perseverance, for afflictions become "light and momentary" relative to eternal weight (2 Corinthians 4 :17). Thus awareness of finite calendar births infinite hope. Regular reflection on birthdays as diminishing returns paradoxically multiplies significance of remaining days, compelling redemptive action.

2.9.2 Liturgy of Lament and Ash-Wednesday Practices

Corporate worship that includes lament permits congregations to voice fragility together, countering triumphalism. Psalms of lament constitute one-third of the psalter, yet many song sets neglect them. Ash Wednesday smears charcoal crosses while uttering, "Remember that you are dust," anchoring penitence in embodiment. Such rituals discipline emotions, teaching believers to weep with those who weep (Romans 12 :15) and to celebrate only after confession. They also catechize children early, integrating mortality into faith rather than shielding them with euphemisms. When pandemic closures shuttered sanctuaries, some pastors distributed ash packets for home imposition, reasserting practice despite inconvenience. Liturgy thus proves adaptable yet essential, embedding mortality within gospel narrative. Through lament, wounds become wombs birthing compassion.

2.9.3 Sabbath Rest as Antidote to Panic

Weekly cessation of labor confesses that the world spins fine without human micromanagement. Israel rested even during harvest (Exodus 34 :21), testifying trust in Provider. Sabbath dismantles idolatry of productivity, which attempts to outrun vulnerability through overtime. Jesus identifies Himself as Lord of the Sabbath (Mark 2 :28), inviting weary souls to rest in His completed work. Practicing Sabbath can involve digital detox, leisurely meals, and worship—countercultural resistance against 24/7 economies. Rest reminds believers that final salvation is "not a result of works" (Ephesians 2 :9). By slowing pulse, Sabbath opens space to hear eternity's whisper. Fear subsides when identity anchors in grace rather than accomplishment.

2.9.4 The Daily Habit of Repentance and Readiness

Martin Luther's first thesis declared that the entire Christian life is repentance. Regular confession keeps accounts short, so sudden death doesn't catch the soul unprepared. Jesus' parable of bridesmaids with oil lamps (Matthew 25 :1-13) urges vigilance; repentance fills flasks with grace. Nightly examen—a review of day's thoughts and actions—allows course corrections before patterns calcify. Early church fathers recommended the Kyrie eleison on waking and sleeping lips. Such rhythms cultivate peace, for "there is now no condemnation for those in Christ" (Romans 8 :1). Readiness also energizes mission, as redeemed joy overflows in witness. Thus, repentance is not mere avoidance of wrath but active participation in life abundant.

Conclusion

Human life resembles a candle flickering in a drafty corridor—beautiful, valuable, yet vulnerable to the slightest gust. History, Scripture, philosophy, and daily headlines harmonize in a single anthem: *creature, remember you are dust.* Yet this acknowledgement is designed not to paralyze but to prioritize, redirecting attention from self-made fortresses to the everlasting arms. Every busted idol, every shattered illusion of control, becomes an invitation to rest in the God who numbers hairs and galaxies alike. The abyss is real, but so is the bridge of redemption stretching across it. Those who heed mortality's sermon will not merely prepare to die; they will learn how to live—generously, repentantly, and watchfully—until the Day when frailty is swallowed up by immortality and the suspended thread is replaced by unbreakable union with Christ.

Chapter 3. The Justice That Makes Wrath Reasonable

The human ache for fairness reverberates across cultures and centuries. We sense instinctively that wrong acts demand redress, whether a child on a playground yelling, "That's not fair!" or an international court indicting war criminals. The Christian Scriptures claim that this shared intuition springs from a Creator who embedded justice into the marrow of the universe. In a cosmos so designed, wrath is not the petulance of a capricious deity but the necessary expression of holiness when confronted with evil. Chapter 3 probes that claim in depth. It traces the moral architecture God built into creation, follows the trajectory of His law through redemptive history, exposes the cosmic treason of sin, and gazes upon the cross where mercy and judgment embrace. Along the way it tackles common objections, clarifies eternal consequences, and shows how the certainty of an impartial tribunal galvanizes both evangelism and daily integrity. What emerges is a picture of justice so pure that it renders divine wrath not only reasonable but inevitable—and of mercy so radiant that it leaves no room for despair.

Prelude - The Universal Cry for Fairness

Conscience as courtroom: why even children protest "That's not fair!" Conscience functions like an internal bench of judges, convened whenever we observe or commit a moral act. Long before toddlers can recite ethical codes, they recognize inequity when a sibling receives a larger cookie, demonstrating that moral categories are woven into human cognition (Romans 2 :14-15). The language of fairness arises spontaneously, not by cultural indoctrination alone. Neurological studies show emotions of moral disgust activating the same brain regions worldwide, suggesting a shared design. When conscience condemns personal wrongdoing, it delivers a verdict combined with an implied sentence—guilt demanding atonement. Attempts to silence that verdict through distraction or rationalization rarely succeed for long; the bench reconvenes in dreams, memories, and mid-night regrets. Thus the very existence of conscience hints that humanity lives under an unseen but objective moral administration. If God authored that interior court, His external judgment is but the public session of a process begun in every heart. Divine wrath therefore harmonizes with, rather than contradicts, our deepest moral instincts.

Historic quests for equity from Hammurabi to modern constitutions Civilizations have always encoded concepts of retribution and recompense. Hammurabi's Babylonian stele etched lex talionis—"eye for eye"—in stone, insisting that punishment match offense. Ancient Israel's Torah refined that principle by placing even kings beneath the same statutes (Deuteronomy 17 :18-20). Greek philosophers sought justice in balanced souls and orderly polities, while Roman jurists built complex systems of contract and tort. Enlightenment thinkers drafted constitutions with checks and balances to scatter power, acknowledging human propensity for tyranny. Each development—however imperfect—signals a shared conviction that a society ignoring justice will devour itself. Yet historical records of slavery, genocide, and corruption prove that human structures falter. They cry out for a final court immune to bribery and bias. Scripture answers with the promise of a day "when God judges the secrets of men by

Christ Jesus" (Romans 2 :16). Divine wrath, then, is not a primitive vestige; it fulfills the long, unfinished project of human jurisprudence.

How moral outrage hints at transcendent standards When news feeds display atrocities, people instinctively declare them evil rather than merely distasteful. Such absolute language presupposes an external moral plumb line. If ethics were wholly relative, outrage would reduce to personal preference, no more binding than taste in music. Yet survivors of injustice rarely find solace in relativism; they hunger for objective vindication. C.S. Lewis observed that arguing about right and wrong is as universal as breathing, and that debate implies a standard transcending both parties. Atheist philosopher J. L. Mackie conceded that moral objectivity would "make more sense" if God existed, even as he denied Him. The Christian contends that God's character supplies that standard, and wrath is the enforcement arm of His perfect legislature. Moral outrage, far from discrediting faith, corroborates it by revealing desires only the biblical narrative fully satisfies. Thus the cry for fairness serves as pre-evangelium, a preparatory melody anticipating the gospel's symphony.

3.1 The Moral Architecture of the Universe

3.1.1 Justice as the radiant facet of divine holiness
Holiness in Scripture is not bare purity but a blazing amalgam of righteousness, beauty, and power (Isaiah 6 :1-3). Justice is holiness translated into relational action, ensuring that goodness is preserved and evil answered. Without justice, holiness would be inert admiration; with justice, it becomes moral light scorching darkness (Psalm 97 :2-6). The psalmist proclaims that righteousness and justice are the very *foundation* of Yahweh's throne (Psalm 89 :14), meaning governance itself rests on equitable decrees. Hence wrath is no afterthought; it is holy love's defensive perimeter, firing whenever creation is threatened by sin's vandalism. A

universe governed by such a Monarch is safe for the oppressed yet terrifying for the oppressor. Understanding wrath as justice's kinetic energy recasts biblical judgments—from Eden's exile to Revelation's bowls—not as divine mood swings but consistent expressions of a throne whose scepter is straight. Thus holiness necessitates justice, and justice, when violated, necessitates wrath.

3.1.2 Law written on human hearts and echoed in natural order (Romans 2 :14-15) Paul argues that even Gentiles without Mosaic revelation perform "by nature" acts aligned with Torah, proving an internal inscription. Anthropologists confirm cross-cultural taboos against murder, theft, and perjury. Nature itself reinforces moral cause-and-effect: sow thistles, reap thorns; sow venom, reap death. Ecological systems punish imbalance, economic markets penalize fraud with collapse, and relational networks fracture under betrayal. These feedback loops whisper that the universe favors righteousness. When societies codify just laws they merely echo deeper grooves etched by the Creator's finger. Hence the conscience's verdict finds external corroboration in creation's rhythms, forming a double witness that renders humankind "without excuse" (Romans 1 :20). Suppressing that witness demands intellectual contortions, but it never fully erases the carved lines.

3.1.3 Cause-and-effect woven into creation: "You reap what you sow" (Galatians 6 :7) Agricultural Israel understood that seeds predict harvest. Paul universalizes the principle: moral actions germinate consequences. Covetousness sown in Achan's tent yielded national defeat (Joshua 7). David's secret adultery sprouted public family chaos (2 Samuel 12-18). Conversely, Joseph's integrity in Potiphar's house ripened into national deliverance (Genesis 41 :39-41). Modern addictions, corporate scandals, and broken marriages continue the pattern. While grace can intercept some crops, sparing sinners from full yield, the farm still teaches that sin's pleasure is seasonal, but its harvest enduring. This embedded law testifies to an unseen Legislator and foreshadows final judgment when every sowing reaps ultimate fruit. Wrath, then, is harvest time escalated to cosmic scale.

3.1.4 Covenant blessings and curses as built-in sanctions (Deuteronomy 28) At Sinai and later on Moab's plains, Yahweh presented Israel with a treaty: obedience would invite rain, fertility, and victory; defiance would trigger famine, disease, and exile. These clauses were not arbitrary punishments but covenantal cause-and-effect grounded in God's character. Blessing upheld creation's order; curse signaled its fracture. Centuries later, prophets interpreted Assyrian raids and Babylonian deportations through this lens, calling the disasters "the Lord's day" of reckoning (Hosea 9 :7). For the church, new-covenant promises shift focus from land to Spirit, yet Paul warns that persistent sin can still invite temporal chastening (1 Corinthians 11 :30-32). The covenant pattern thus persists: justice woven into divine relationships, with wrath as covenant lawsuit when terms are violated.

3.2 Holy Law in the Storyline of Redemption

3.2.1 Sinai statutes: protecting life, liberty, and land The Ten Commandments carve two tablets: love for God and neighbor (Exodus 20 :1-17). Subsequent case laws translate principles into daily life—ox-gore restitution safeguards bodily dignity; gleaning mandates honor the poor; Sabbath rest equalizes masters and servants. Far from repressive, Torah erects fences around flourishing. Its repeated refrain, "I am the LORD," links each statute to covenant love. Violating the law therefore affronts both community and covenant partner. When Israel disobeys, prophets call the breach not merely illegality but adultery. Thus law is relationally charged—justice with a personal face. Understanding wrath demands reading it as injured Husband defending marital vows.

3.2.2 Prophetic lawsuits: Yahweh arraigns His people (Isaiah 1; Micah 6) Courtroom imagery saturates prophetic oracles: heavens and earth are summoned as witnesses;

indictments list idolatry and oppression; verdicts pronounce siege and exile. Isaiah opens with God lamenting rebellious children whose worship masks blood-stained hands (Isaiah 1 :2-15). Micah frames a covenant lawsuit, asking what Yahweh requires—justice, mercy, humility (Micah 6 :1-8). These scenes reveal wrath as judicial, not explosive. God presents evidence, offers plea bargains of repentance, and only then executes sentence. Such procedure underscores reasonableness; no defendant suffers without trial. In the gospel, the trial climaxes with charges transferred onto Christ, showing that justice is satisfied even when mercy triumphs.

3.2.3 Wisdom literature and poetic retribution (Proverbs 11 :1; Psalm 73)

Proverbs links ethical conduct to concrete outcomes: dishonest scales provoke divine abhorrence, whereas generosity enlarges soul and storehouse. These observations are empirical yet theocentric—patterns reflecting Creator governance. Psalm 73 wrestles when the wicked appear to prosper, but resolves within sanctuary where ultimate destinies clarify justice: slippery paths end in ruin. Wisdom texts thus balance immediate cause-and-effect with eschatological correction, affirming that any temporal discrepancy will be righted. Wrath, seen through wisdom's lens, is delayed retribution rather than denied. Therefore believers embrace righteousness even when dividends seem deferred, trusting the Judge of all the earth to do right (Genesis 18 :25).

3.2.4 Jesus intensifies, not relaxes, the law (Matthew 5 :17-48)

In the Sermon on the Mount, Jesus fulfils Torah by revealing its heart-level intent. Anger equals murder in seed form; lust equals adultery incubating in imagination. Far from diluting justice, He magnifies it until every listener stands convicted. Yet He simultaneously reveals Himself as fulfiller who embodies perfect obedience. By demanding righteousness exceeding that of scribes, He drives hearers toward divine provision. Thus wrath becomes reasonable, for holiness now evaluates not merely acts but motives. Grace likewise becomes magnificent, for the same Judge will bear the penalty law requires. Calvary therefore cannot be read apart from Sinai; one explains the severity, the other the substitution.

3.3 Sin as Cosmic High Treason

3.3.1 From "missing the mark" to personal mutiny against Majesty Common catechisms define sin as "any want of conformity unto, or transgression of, the law of God," but Scripture layers rebellion imagery atop legal jargon. Jeremiah calls sin "forsaking the fountain of living waters" (Jeremiah 2 :13); Isaiah pictures revolt against a benevolent sovereign (Isaiah 1 :2). The prodigal son's departure insults paternal dignity, while tenants who beat the landowner's servants commit treason (Luke 20 :9-16). Each metaphor raises guilt from technical misstep to relational betrayal. To rob a peasant is crime; to assault a king is treason multiplied by throne's glory. Thus, when finite creatures defy the Infinite, the offense takes on immeasurable weight, warranting wrath proportional to the dignity violated.

3.3.2 Infinite offense against infinite worth: why gravity escalates God's value is unbounded; therefore any affront, however momentary, assumes infinite seriousness. A slap to a stranger incurs misdemeanor; the same to a head of state triggers national crisis. How much more when the offended party sustains galaxies by His word. Jonathan Edwards argued that the duration of punishment depends not on the time required to commit the act but on the magnitude of the dishonor. Hence eternal consequence does not exaggerate guilt; it mirrors the offended Majesty's worth. Rejecting this logic diminishes divine glory to manageable proportions. If punishment appears excessive, the real issue may be our underestimation of God's holiness, not His overreaction.

3.3.3 Adamic solidarity and inherited guilt (Romans 5 :12-19) Paul teaches that sin invaded through one man, and death through sin, spreading to all because all sinned. Corporate identity offends modern individualism, yet every society shares liabilities—national debt, polluted air. Adam functioned as covenant head; his fall enrolled descendants in bankruptcy. We confirm inheritance by personal transgression, proving affinity with first father. Thus wrath addresses both root and fruit, nature and acts. In Christ, a new head offers righteousness crediting many. Understanding solidarity enlarges justice: God deals with humanity not as isolated atoms but as relational network, and His remedy matches the structure of the ruin.

3.3.4 Structural evil: systems that multiply personal rebellion Sin metastasizes from hearts to institutions: Pharaoh's brick quotas, Jezebel's idol policies, modern trafficking rings. Isaiah condemns those who "make unjust laws" that rob the poor (Isaiah 10 :1-2). Revelation personifies empire as Babylon, drunk on saints' blood (Revelation 17). Systemic evil complicates justice, for victims suffer beyond their own choices. God's wrath accounts for this complexity, targeting rulers and structures. The cross dismantles dividing walls, birthing a kingdom of righteousness that challenges oppressive systems. Christians engaged in social reform thus act as agents of the coming judgment, previewing a world where righteousness dwells (2 Peter 3 :13).

3.4 The Cross: Confluence of Justice and Mercy

3.4.1 A survey of atonement theories with legal satisfaction at the core Ransom imagery pictures Christus Victor liberating captives; moral-influence theory emphasizes love's demonstration; yet beneath each lies judicial satisfaction—sin-debt paid (Colossians 2 :14). Anselm argued that only a God-man could render honor commensurate with offense. Reformers sharpened penal substitution, citing Isaiah 53 :5, "He was pierced for our transgressions." Modern critiques fear divine child abuse, but Scripture portrays Trinitarian self-giving, not coercive patriarchy. Whatever subsidiary motifs enrich atonement, legal satisfaction anchors them; without it, liberation lacks courtroom declaration, and moral example lacks remedy. Therefore justice defines mercy's boundary, ensuring that grace does not sabotage righteousness.

3.4.2 "The cup," "the curse," and "the ransom" as judicial metaphors

In Gethsemane Jesus dreads a cup steeped in wrathful wine (Jeremiah 25 :15-17). On Golgotha He hangs under Deuteronomy's curse, "cursed is everyone who is hanged on a tree" (Galatians 3 :13). He also calls His life a ransom for many (Mark 10 :45), echoing Exodus redemption price. Each term implies judicial exchange: liability assumed, penalty discharged. Far from contradicting Fatherly love, these metaphors showcase its cost. Divine justice is not sidelined but exhausted, allowing mercy to flow freely without legal compromise. Thus Calvary stands as the cosmic courthouse where gavel fell on sin and rose in resurrection vindication.

3.4.3 Penal substitution and divine Fatherhood held in harmony (Romans 3 :25-26)

Paul declares God set forth Christ as propitiation to demonstrate righteousness, so He might be just *and* justifier. That conjunction prevents envisioning God at war with Himself; rather, justice and love harmonize within the Godhead. The Father does not punish an unwilling Son; the Son willingly offers Himself in Spirit's power (Hebrews 9 :14). Family imagery persists even at the cross: "My God, My God" presupposes relationship strained but not severed. Thus penal substitution intensifies rather than diminishes Fatherhood—it shows love stout enough to bear law's full brunt for children's adoption. Wrath satisfied magnifies tenderness displayed.

3.4.4 Resurrection as the public verdict of righteous vindication

If death were wages fully paid, Christ's empty tomb is receipt stamped "paid in full." God "raised Him for our justification" (Romans 4 :25), announcing acceptance of substitute. Resurrection therefore belongs within legal narrative—acquittal broadcast to cosmos. It also validates future judgment, for God has fixed a day to judge by the Man He raised (Acts 17 :31). Believers thus face tribunal not as defendants but witnesses, their verdict pre-released in Easter dawn. Justice underwrites assurance; because wrath fell, peace stands. Hence evangelists preach not only crucified but risen Savior, combining courtroom victory with kingdom inauguration.

3.5 The Reasonableness of Eternal Consequence

3.5.1 Finite acts, infinite Person offended: proportional logic explored Critics argue that endless punishment for finite sin is disproportionate. Yet duration of penalty often correlates with value of principle breached, not time of offense. Perjury seconds can earn years; treason minutes can merit life sentences. Eternal God's worth elevates offense beyond temporal metrics. Moreover, sin's effects ripple unendingly; a false teaching may damn generations (James 3 :1). Therefore perpetual consequence mirrors ongoing harm and infinite affront. Grace offered yet refused intensifies guilt, for light rejected is darkness chosen. Justice respects human freedom enough to ratify its final preference.

3.5.2 Self-bending will and the ongoing posture of rejection (Revelation 22 :11) John closes Apocalypse with a chilling admonition: "Let the evildoer still do evil ... and the righteous still do right." Character solidifies into eternity; hell's residents persist in rebellion, compounding guilt. C.S. Lewis described doors locked from the inside. Thus punishment is not merely retributive but consequential—experiencing life apart from God one insisted upon. The will, once curved inward (*incurvatus in se*), spirals deeper without grace infusion. Therefore hell's duration aligns with unceasing impenitence. God's wrath remains reasonable, for it ratifies the sinner's chosen allegiance.

3.5.3 Degrees of punishment: "many stripes, few stripes" (Luke 12 :47-48) Jesus teaches that servants aware of master's will yet disobey merit severe beating, while ignorant ones receive lighter. Paul speaks of wrath storing up "for the day" (Romans 2 :5), implying calibrated measurement. Such gradation answers criticism that eternal judgment flattens moral distinctions. While all outside Christ perish, not all experience identical woe. Divine omniscience ensures perfect proportionality—facts, motives, context weighed. Hence the doctrine elevates justice, preserving nuance beyond human courts. Believers moved by compassion can rest that no atrocity will escape fitting response, nor will lesser faults incur excessive penalty.

3.5.4 Hell's imagery—fire, darkness, exclusion— explained juridically Metaphors converge, each highlighting an aspect of penalty: fire signals torment and purification; darkness conveys isolation; outer exile depicts banishment from covenant celebration (Matthew 8 :12). Collectively they portray holistic loss—physical, relational, spiritual. Legal banishment in ancient Israel foreshadowed this: lepers quarantined, murderers expelled to cities of refuge. Jesus borrows Gehenna, Jerusalem's refuse valley, symbolizing final disposal of all that defiles. These images are not scare tactics but juridical descriptions scaled to cosmic gravity. If blindness to glory is the essence of damnation, then darkness fits. If sin corrupts creation, incineration cleanses. Thus wrath's visuals carry courtroom logic, not primitive sadism.

3.6 Contemporary Objections and Christian Apologetic

3.6.1 "Why not immediate justice?"—divine patience and common grace Skeptics sit under evil's shadow and ask why lightning does not strike perpetrators instantly. Peter answers: the Lord is patient, "not wishing that any should perish but that all should reach repentance" (2 Peter 3 :9). Delay is mercy, extending amnesty; meanwhile, common grace restrains utter chaos, sending rain on just and unjust (Matthew 5 :45). Courts also require investigation before verdict; God's omniscience could judge immediately, but His fatherly heart prefers reconciliation. Patience, therefore, coexists with justice, not contradicting it. Every sunset grants sinners more time to surrender, leaving none to complain of insufficient opportunity.

3.6.2 Distinguishing holy wrath from capricious human anger Human anger often springs from wounded pride or ignorance. Divine wrath is measured, purposeful, and perfectly informed (James 1 :20). Unlike pagan deities subject to mood swings, Yahweh's anger operates within covenant, after warnings, and aims at restoration. Even severe judgments—Noah's flood, Sodom's fire—allow escape routes for the righteous. When Christians display spite or vindictiveness, they misrepresent God; the cross remains the calibration tool, showing wrath embraced by love. Apologetics must emphasize this qualitative difference or risk projecting human flaws onto heaven's throne.

3.6.3 Free will, determinism, and moral accountability in dialogue Philosophers debate whether divine sovereignty undermines responsibility. Scripture upholds both: God works all things after counsel of His will (Ephesians 1 :11), yet summons people to choose life (Deuteronomy 30 :19). Compatibilism offers a framework: choices are free when springing from desires, and desires operate under God's providence. Judgment assesses what people *want*, not what they are coerced to do, rendering wrath just. Romans 9 anticipates objections, asserting that potter's rights coexist with creaturely accountability. Pastoral emphasis lies not in solving metaphysical puzzles but in proclaiming mercy available now, leaving secret things to God (Deuteronomy 29 :29).

3.6.4 Universalism, annihilationism, and the ethics of exclusion Universalists hope all will eventually be saved, citing God's desire that none perish. Yet texts of exclusion— sheep vs. goats (Matthew 25 :31-46), narrow gate (Luke 13 :24)—persist. Annihilationists argue that loving God would not sustain torment, but Revelation's "smoke forever" resists. Ethically, eternal hell warns oppressors and consoles victims, preventing vigilantism. If evil ends in non-existence with no reckoning, moral equilibrium falters. Thus orthodox doctrine, while sobering, safeguards ethics by affirming that choices matter eternally. Apologists must present these views humbly, acknowledging emotional weight while honoring biblical testimony.

3.7 Justice as Evangelistic Motivation

3.7.1 The missionary impulse of impending judgment (Acts 17 :30-31) Paul tells Athenians that God commands repentance because He appointed a day to judge the world by a risen Man. Judgment furnishes urgency; without it, evangelism devolves into lifestyle enhancement. Historical revivals—from Wesleyan itinerancy to Korean awakenings— flamed when pulpits preached both cross and crown. Missionaries endure hardship, knowing divine court will vindicate sacrifices. Every unreached people group represents souls poised before bar of justice, compelling translation work and church planting. Hell fuels compassion, not triumphalism, for evangelists are beggars telling beggars where bread is.

3.7.2 Partnering social justice with eschatological hope Christians tackling trafficking or poverty do so believing God hates oppression. Future judgment promises perpetrators will face recompense, empowering activists to labor without despair. Social work divorced from eschatology risks burnout; conversely, eschatology divorced from social work breeds passivity. Scripture weds them: Amos pairs coming darkness with demands for justice to roll like waters (Amos 5 :24). Thus gospel proclamation and social reform dance together, each fueled by vision of righteous kingdom.

3.7.3 Preaching law to prepare hearts for grace, Edwards to today Jonathan Edwards spent two-thirds of sermons diagnosing sin before prescribing remedy. Law plows soil; grace plants seed. Modern preaching often reverses order, sowing onto untilled ground, yielding shallow roots. Articulating justice awakens conscience dulled by relativism. Yet tone matters: tears accompany warnings. Jesus wept over Jerusalem while predicting its ruin (Luke 19 :41-44). Shepherds who weep convey authenticity, making wrath credible and grace irresistible.

3.7.4 Pastoral care for victims awaiting divine vindication (Revelation 6 :9-11) Martyred souls cry, "How long?" Pastors echo heaven's reassurance: judgment will

come. Victims of abuse need to hear that God saw and will repay, freeing them from revenge's poison. Lament psalms legitimize anger while entrusting outcome to Divine Judge (Psalm 10). Communities practicing Church discipline preview this vindication, removing predators and protecting lambs. Such care images eschatological shepherd who will wipe tears and right wrongs.

3.8 Living Justly Before the Coming Tribunal

3.8.1 Personal integrity: honest scales and truthful lips
Proverbs denounces dishonest weights (Proverbs 11 :1). In contemporary terms: accurate resumes, transparent taxes, genuine online personas. Believers aware of omniscient audit reject shortcuts. Joseph shunned adultery because "How then could I do this great wickedness and sin against God?" (Genesis 39 :9). Integrity becomes worship—life offered as living sacrifice. Such consistency commends gospel to skeptical observers more than slogans.

3.8.2 Forgiving enemies without trivializing wrongs (Romans 12 :19-21) Paul commands believers to leave vengeance to God, yet also overcome evil with good. Assurance of divine justice frees hearts from resentment. Forgiveness does not excuse offense; it transfers case to higher court. Corrie ten Boom testified to flash of grace enabling handshake with former guard, fueled by knowledge that Christ bore or will bear that man's sin. Thus eschatology empowers radical reconciliation while maintaining moral seriousness.

3.8.3 Church discipline as micro-court previewing macro judgment Matthew 18 outlines process: private rebuke, plural confirmation, public censure. Its goal is restoration, reflecting God's reluctance to condemn. Excommunication treats unrepentant members as outsiders, foreshadowing final separation. When practiced humbly, discipline trains saints to judge angels (1 Corinthians 6 :2-3)

and warns sinners of real peril. Neglect of discipline breeds scandal, undermining church witness and cheapening grace.

3.8.4 Anticipating the Bema Seat: rewards and loss for believers (1 Corinthians 3 :12-15) Paul envisions believers' works tested by fire: gold endures, straw incinerates. Salvation remains, but reward varies. Thus justice motivates excellence—craft sermons well, code software ethically, raise children faithfully. Crowns bestowed become instruments of worship, cast before throne (Revelation 4 :10). Hope of commendation—"Well done, good and faithful servant" (Matthew 25 :21)—enlivens mundane tasks with eternal significance.

Conclusion

Divine wrath is trustworthy because it flows from a justice older than stars and deeper than seas—a justice that defends oppressed, condemns oppressor, and refuses to negotiate truth. Far from contradicting love, it proves love's integrity, for affection that never confronts evil is sentimental fraud. In Jesus Christ, justice reached climactic expression: the Lawgiver absorbed law's penalty so lawbreakers could become heirs. The cross therefore silences every objection, shattering the myth of arbitrary anger and unveiling a holiness both terrifying and tender. Those who embrace this revelation find themselves liberated from vengeance, energized for mission, and eager for the day when the Judge will set the universe to rights. Until then, every heartbeat echoes a summons: live justly, love mercy, and walk humbly with the God who has sworn to let no injustice stand unaddressed.

Chapter 4. The Folly of False Assurance

No peril is more subtle—and therefore more lethal—than a false sense of spiritual security. Multitudes drift toward eternity convinced that a few religious credentials will suffice before the tribunal of the Holy One. Yet Scripture's pages are strewn with warnings against misplaced confidence, from Israel chanting "the temple of the LORD" while plotting injustice (Jer 7 :1-11) to smug Laodiceans who crowed "I am rich" while heaven saw them naked and blind (Rev 3 :17-18). False assurance is the velvet pillow that lulls a sinner on the very edge of the precipice. It anesthetizes conscience, muffles the Spirit's alarms, and converts the gospel's urgent summons into background noise. This chapter exposes the anatomy of counterfeit comfort, tracing its expressions through nominal religion, moralistic pride, perverted grace, icy orthodoxy, emotional hype, prosperity delusions, and corporate self-deception. It then unfolds biblical tests of authentic conversion and pastoral strategies for awakening the self-assured. Our aim is not to foster morbid introspection but to drive every reader toward the only refuge that can bear the weight of eternity—the crucified and risen Christ.

Prelude - When Confidence Becomes Catastrophe

The deceptive calm before spiritual disaster Storm clouds often gather beyond the horizon while a deceptive stillness lingers over the sea; likewise, souls on the brink of judgment may feel serenely untroubled. Israel prospered under Jeroboam II, expanding borders and enjoying affluence even as Amos announced imminent exile (Am 6 :1-7). The deception springs from measuring peace by circumstances instead of covenant standing, forgetting that patience is not approval but mercy holding back the tide. Such calm blunts urgency, persuading sinners that warnings are exaggerated or pertain only to notorious offenders. Jesus compares the final day to Noah's age when people ate, drank, married, and built until waters erupted (Matt 24 :37-39). Superficial tranquility thus betrays rather than blesses, masking cracks that widen under foot. Recognizing this dynamic is vital, for an untroubled conscience can be the quiet before the soul's quake. Only truth strong enough to pierce illusions can prevent catastrophe.

Biblical portraits of self-deceived religionists The Scriptures bristle with characters whose self-confidence proved fatal. Cain worshiped but nursed envy and fell under curse (Gen 4 :3-12). Nadab and Abihu offered strange fire with priestly robes still fresh and died before the altar (Lev 10 :1-3). Saul swore loyalty to Yahweh while sparing Amalekite spoil and forfeited his throne (1 Sam 15 :13-23). New-Testament counterparts abound: Judas healed the sick yet sold his Master; Diotrephes loved preeminence and opposed apostolic authority (3 John 9-10). Each story exposes common threads—ritual performed without obedience, authority assumed without submission, words of orthodoxy masking hearts of rebellion. Scripture preserves these tragedies not for morbid curiosity but as cautionary road signs. They shout across millennia that spiritual privilege can harden rather than humble if unaccompanied by repentance. Heeding these portraits readies the heart to distrust surface impressions and seek authentic grace.

Why counterfeit comfort is more dangerous than open rebellion Open rebels at least recognize their alienation and may feel the pangs of conscience that lead to repentance, as did the prodigal in the far country (Luke 15 :17-18). Counterfeit believers, however, vaccinate themselves with a diluted gospel, receiving just enough religion to render them immune to the real cure. Jesus said tax collectors and prostitutes were entering the kingdom ahead of self-righteous clergy because outcasts sensed their need (Matt 21 :31-32). False assurance dulls perception, making warnings seem irrelevant; it also breeds spiritual pride that resents any hint of deficiency. Moreover, self-deception can infest entire communities, reinforcing complacency through mutual congratulation. Thus counterfeit comfort resembles carbon-monoxide: odorless, painless, silently lethal. Only the Spirit's detector—the living, active word—can pierce the haze and trigger alarm. Exposing this danger is therefore an act of mercy, not of condemnation.

4.1 Nominal Faith and Empty Ritual

4.1.1 Cultural Christianity: inherited religion without regeneration In many contexts the faith is transmitted like a surname—received at birth, displayed on census forms, yet seldom examined. Cultural Christians attend seasonal services, quote familiar psalms at funerals, and list "Christian" on social-media profiles, but cannot articulate personal repentance or the new birth Jesus declares indispensable (John 3 :3-7). Their attachment is sociological, not salvific; it confers belonging and moral respectability while demanding little transformation. The danger surfaces when such individuals mistake heritage for heart change, assuming baptismal certificates or denominational pedigrees guarantee entry into the kingdom. Paul's anguish for kinsmen "having a form of godliness but denying its power" (2 Tim 3 :5) applies. Nominalism inoculates against conviction: any preacher's call to repentance sounds like a message for "outsiders." Only a Spirit-wrought encounter that turns inherited creed into living

reality can rupture this veneer and awaken genuine discipleship.

4.1.2 Sacraments as talismans: when symbols eclipse reality Baptism and the Lord's Supper are covenant signs meant to nourish faith, yet history shows how easily they morph into magical rites. Medieval Europe sprinkled infants by state decree, producing legions of unconverted parishioners who trusted the font more than the cross. Corinthian believers treated Eucharist casually and suffered judgment (1 Cor 11 :27-30), illustrating that participation without discernment provokes, rather than averts, wrath. When symbols eclipse the realities they signify, worshipers begin to trust water, bread, and wine as automatic grace dispensers. Such sacramentalism fosters spiritual sloth—no need for ongoing repentance if ritual has mechanically cleansed. Scripture counters that circumcision of heart, not flesh, marks God's people (Rom 2 :28-29). Properly received, sacraments point beyond themselves to Christ's finished work; misused, they function like lucky charms, shielding the soul from the very grace they symbolize.

4.1.3 The peril of presuming on covenant identity (Jeremiah 7 :1-11) Jeremiah stood at the temple gate and thundered against worshipers who chanted "the temple of the LORD" while committing theft, adultery, and oppression. They assumed God's house guaranteed God's favor, turning sacred space into a "den of robbers." Their error lay in confusing privilege with immunity—believing election negated accountability. Paul later warns Gentile converts not to boast, for natural branches were broken off Israel's olive tree through unbelief (Rom 11 :17-22). Presumption converts covenant promises into pillows for sin, distorting grace into entitlement. True covenant identity manifests in obedience born of faith, not mere proximity to holy things. The prophetic indictment therefore speaks to every baptized but unconverted churchgoer: do not mistake access to ordinances for assurance of salvation.

4.1.4 Diagnosing lifeless liturgy in contemporary worship Modern congregations can repeat creeds, project lyrics, and stage flawless productions while souls remain untouched by holiness. When songs become performance and sermons motivational pep-talks, worship devolves into weekly entertainment. The church in Sardis had a reputation for being alive yet was dead (Rev 3 :1-3), proving that polished externals can mask decay. Diagnostic questions probe: Does liturgy lead to confession of sin and awe of Christ, or merely affirm self-esteem? Do members pursue holiness Monday through Saturday, or compartmentalize faith to weekend rituals? The cure is not abandoning structure but infusing it with gospel gravity—scripture readings that wound and heal, prayers of lament and adoration, sacraments framed by repentance and faith. Only when liturgy becomes encounter rather than routine will empty forms pulse with life.

4.2 Moralism Masquerading as Salvation

4.2.1 The limits of ethical reformation (Luke 18 :9-14)
Jesus contrasts a Pharisee boasting of fasting and tithing with a tax collector begging mercy. The parable shatters the assumption that moral polish secures justification. Ethical reform can curb societal decay, but it cannot erase guilt or impart new hearts. Like painting a gravestone, it beautifies death. Israel attempted righteousness by law but stumbled because they pursued it apart from faith (Rom 9 :31-33). Moralism leads to either pride or despair: pride when one succeeds, despair when failure appears. The gospel offers a third way—imputed righteousness received by trust, producing gratitude-fueled obedience. Until a sinner owns helplessness, good deeds remain filthy rags (Isa 64 :6). Thus ethical improvement, though commendable, is eternally insufficient.

4.2.2 Self-righteous scoring systems and selective obedience
Humans craft private scorecards that rank sins like gossip lower than scandal while exalting virtues that match personal strengths. Pharisees tithed mint and cumin yet neglected justice and mercy (Matt 23 :23). Modern equivalents include abstaining from smoking while harboring bitterness, or championing social causes while indulging sexual immorality.

Such selective obedience maintains illusion of goodness by ignoring commandments that pierce cherished idols. James insists that breaking one point of law makes a transgressor of all (Jas 2 :10-11). God's standard is wholeness—loving Him with all heart, soul, mind, and strength. Any homemade scale that passes self-inspection but fails divine audit is folly. True holiness embraces the full counsel of God, empowered by grace rather than self-effort.

4.2.3 Virtue signaling versus Spirit-wrought holiness In the age of social media, righteousness often displays itself in hashtags and profile banners. Virtue signaling garners applause without costly action, feeding ego while avoiding sacrifice. Jesus warned of practicing righteousness to be seen by others; such performers "have received their reward" (Matt 6 :1-5). Spirit-wrought holiness, in contrast, flows from inward transformation, seeks God's approval, and persists when no audience cheers. It forgives in secret, gives anonymously, and endures misunderstanding. Paul labored more abundantly yet attributed effort to grace (1 Cor 15 :10), demonstrating humility absent from self-promotion. Distinguishing the two motivations requires heart scrutiny under the Spirit's light, for external acts may look identical. Only fruit borne from abiding in Christ glorifies the Father (John 15 :5-8).

4.2.4 When "good enough" becomes eternally fatal Many assume God grades on a curve, weighing good deeds against bad. Proverbs 14 :12 counters: "There is a way that seems right to a man, but its end is the way to death." Rich young ruler claimed perfect law-keeping yet lacked one thing— relinquishing idols to follow Jesus (Mark 10 :17-22). One fatal gap cancels all other merits, just as chain snapped at a single link drops climber into abyss. The law's purpose is to silence boasting and drive sinners to Christ (Rom 3 :19-20). Relying on "good enough" is like trusting a spiderweb to stop a falling rock; it offers momentary resistance before inevitable collapse. Eternal life demands perfect righteousness, available only in the Son. Rejecting that gift for personal effort ensures eternal loss.

4.3 Perverted Views of Grace

4.3.1 Cheap grace and antinomian distortions (Jude 4)
Jude exposes intruders who turn grace into license for immorality, denying the Master who bought them. Cheap grace divorces pardon from discipleship, picturing God as indulgent grandfather who shrugs at sin. Such teaching tramples Christ's blood, ignoring Paul's question: "Shall we continue in sin that grace may abound?" (Rom 6 :1-2). True grace liberates from sin's penalty and power, training believers to renounce ungodliness (Titus 2 :11-12). Antinomianism promises freedom but delivers slavery; Jesus warned that whoever commits sin is its slave (John 8 :34). Recovering biblical grace involves embracing both justification and sanctification—status and transformation—secured by the same cross. Anything less is counterfeit currency.

4.3.2 Hyper-presumption: "once prayed, forever secure"
Some reduce salvation to reciting a prayer, stamping eternal destiny without evidence of new birth. While Scripture teaches perseverance of true saints, it also insists that faith proves itself through endurance (Heb 3 :14). John writes that those who abandon fellowship reveal they were never of us (1 John 2 :19). Assurance rooted solely in past words yet devoid of present fruit resembles a dormant seed that never sprouts. Jesus says branches not abiding in Him are gathered and burned (John 15 :6). A genuine conversion prayer springboards lifelong repentance and reliance, not complacent indifference. Hyper-presumption lulls professing believers into neglecting means of grace—word, sacrament, community—where assurance matures.

4.3.3 Misusing assurance texts while ignoring warning texts
Passages like John 10 :28 promise no one can snatch believers from Christ's hand, yet Hebrews 10 :26-31 warns persistent rebels of fearful judgment. Scripture balances comfort and caution, but selective readers clutch promises, dismissing admonitions as hypothetical. This imbalance mirrors Satan's misuse of Psalm 91 when tempting Jesus (Matt 4 :6-7). Proper hermeneutics interpret texts within whole-Bible harmony: warnings function as means God uses

to preserve saints. Ignoring them undermines that purpose. The wise heart welcomes both blanket of security and guardrail of exhortation, knowing the Spirit weaves them together to guide pilgrims home.

4.3.4 The gospel that liberates yet binds to joyful obedience Paul describes gospel grace not only saving but teaching believers to live self-controlled, upright, godly lives (Titus 2 :11-14). Freedom from condemnation births freedom to obey; love replaces fear as motive. James calls the law "perfect law of liberty" (Jas 1 :25) because Spirit-filled hearts delight in God's will. Thus grace neither relaxes standards nor burdens with legalism; it infuses power to fulfill righteous requirements the law alone demanded (Rom 8 :3-4). False assurance severs this link, offering liberty without loyalty. Authentic assurance secures identity while stimulating holiness, producing disciples who sing with David, "I run in the path of Your commands, for You have set my heart free" (Ps 119 :32).

4.4 Doctrinal Orthodoxy Without Relational Reality

4.4.1 Demons' faith: correct beliefs, condemned hearts (James 2 :19) James shocks complacent churchgoers by noting demons affirm monotheism yet tremble under judgment. Intellectual assent to creeds cannot save; Nicodemus possessed theological acumen but needed rebirth (John 3 :10-15). Orthodoxy is essential, for truth sets free, yet truth unaccompanied by trust leaves the soul barren. Pharisees sat in Moses' seat, expounding scripture while plotting murder, proving doctrine can coexist with depravity. Saving faith involves personal reliance, surrendering self-rule to Christ's lordship. Believers cherish doctrine because they love the Author, not merely the ideas. When affection dries, orthodoxy becomes museum artifact, admired but powerless.

4.4.2 Idolatry of precision: theology as badge, not transformation Some believers wield doctrinal minutiae like club or trophy, finding identity in nuanced positions rather than union with Christ. Paul warns knowledge puffs up, but love builds (1 Cor 8 :1). Theological tribes may obsess over secondary debates, scorning less informed saints, reproducing Corinthian party spirit. While precision guards against error, idolizing it breeds arrogance and division, antithetical to gospel humility. True doctrine conforms hearts to Christ's character, producing gentleness even amid controversy (2 Tim 2 :24-26). Exegetical accuracy is vital, but if it fails to incinerate pride and inflame worship, it degenerates into dead orthodoxy—beautifully structured tomb.

4.4.3 Prideful gate-keeping and sectarian smugness Jesus rebuked lawyers who withheld knowledge, neither entering kingdom nor allowing others (Luke 11 :52). Modern gate-keepers patrol doctrinal borders with suspicion, defining identity by what they oppose. Sectarian smugness magnifies minor distinctives, implying outsiders cannot possibly belong to God's people. Paul lamented that some preached Christ to afflict him, yet he rejoiced the gospel advanced (Phil 1 :15-18). A humble orthodoxy guards truth while celebrating Christ's work beyond tribal lines. When pride erects walls taller than cross, the movement risks becoming cultish echo chamber. Gospel-shaped communities hold firm essentials, extend charity in non-essentials, and pursue unity in love.

4.4.4 Word and Spirit united: truth aflame with love Pentecost married sound exposition—Peter's scriptural sermon—with Spirit-empowered conviction, birthing a church devoted to apostolic teaching and fellowship (Acts 2 :41-47). Orthodoxy divorced from Spirit yields dryness; spiritual zeal minus truth breeds wildfire. Jesus insists true worshipers worship in spirit and truth (John 4 :23-24). Word supplies framework, Spirit supplies fire; together they forge living encounter. Churches must pray for both articulate preaching and manifest presence, cultivating study and supplication. When union occurs, doctrine sings, and affection deepens, safeguarding against false assurance rooted in intellectualism alone.

4.5 Emotional Enthusiasm and Fleeting Experiences

4.5.1 Shallow soil hearers in Jesus' parable (Matthew 13 :20-21) Seed sown on rocky ground springs up quickly with joy but lacks root; when heat arrives, it withers. Jesus interprets heat as tribulation or persecution exposing depth. Emotional conversions marked by tears and raised hands may signal genuine work, yet without root—doctrine, community, spiritual disciplines—zeal evaporates. Crowds hailed Christ on Palm Sunday and cried "Crucify" by Friday, demonstrating fickle enthusiasm. Feelings, though valuable, are unreliable gauges of regeneration. True joy persists beneath sorrow, anchored in covenant promises rather than fluctuating moods. Gospel preachers must therefore pair invitation with instruction, ensuring new shoots burrow into soil of truth.

4.5.2 Conference highs and Monday morning hollows
Retreats and worship concerts often generate mountaintop experiences where attendees vow radical change. Yet the glow fades when ordinary routines resume—deadlines, diapers, doubts. Elijah's Carmel triumph dissolved into desert despair (1 Kings 19 :3-4), reminding that dramatic encounters must translate into daily obedience. Without structures—accountability groups, devotional habits—euphoria dissipates. The temptation then is to chase the next event, cultivating addiction to adrenaline rather than steady communion. Hebrews exhorts believers to encourage one another daily (Heb 3 :13), maintaining heart warmth between gatherings. Spiritual maturity values ordinary means—word, prayer, fellowship—as embers sustaining lifelong flame.

4.5.3 Distinguishing Spirit fire from soul flash-paper
Jonathan Edwards, analyzing the Great Awakening, noted that genuine revival elevates esteem for Christ, deepens repentance, and produces lasting fruit. Counterfeit excitement exalts personalities, enflames imagination, and fades quickly. Test every spirit: does it magnify Jesus, honor scripture, humble sinners, and foster holiness (1 John 4 :1-3)? Like flash-paper, emotional hype ignites brightly but leaves no

residue; Spirit fire warms long after spectacle ends. Healthy churches welcome affections yet evaluate them by truth, ensuring experience leads to obedience. Such discernment prevents false assurance built on goosebumps rather than gospel.

4.5.4 Cultivating durable joy through rooted discipleship
Durable joy resembles a tree planted by streams, yielding fruit in season and withstanding drought (Ps 1 :3). Roots sink through meditation on Scripture, prayer, sacrificial service, and trials endured with faith. Paul, chained yet singing, exemplifies joy immune to circumstance (Phil 4 :4-13). Discipleship pathways—one-to-one mentoring, catechism, spiritual disciplines—anchor converts. Suffering, rather than threatening assurance, proves genuineness, for tested faith works endurance (Jas 1 :2-4). As roots deepen, emotional experience becomes steady affection for Christ, resisting storms of doubt. False assurance withers; true assurance thrives in patient cultivation.

4.6 Prosperity and Earthly Success as Divine Approval

4.6.1 Rich fool logic: bigger barns and smaller souls (Luke 12 :16-21) Jesus' parable depicts a farmer congratulating himself on bumper crops, planning leisure, yet dying that night. Wealth fostered illusion of invincibility while masking spiritual poverty—he was "not rich toward God." Prosperity can insulate from perceived need, muffling dependency prayer. Churches in affluent regions risk equating budgets and buildings with God's blessing. Yet Smyrna, materially poor, received no rebuke, while opulent Laodicea nauseated Christ (Rev 2-3). Scripture never condemns riches outright but warns that love of money chokes word (1 Tim 6 :9-10). Evaluating divine favor by bank balance invites catastrophic misreading of providence.

4.6.2 Suffering saints and the upside-down kingdom From Abel to Zechariah, righteous suffer while wicked flourish, challenging simplistic retribution theology. Jesus pronounced blessed the poor, mourning, persecuted, promising kingdom inheritance (Matt 5 :3-12). Paul's apostleship bore marks of lashes and shipwrecks, yet he considered afflictions light compared with glory (2 Cor 11 :23-28; 4 :17). Prosperity gospel thus clashes with biblical pattern: crowns follow crosses, not precede. Believers interpret adversity not as lack of faith but fellowship with Christ's sufferings (Phil 3 :10-11). Any assurance tethered to comfort collapses when trials arrive; assurance founded on union with the Man of Sorrows endures.

4.6.3 Temporal blessing, eternal bankruptcy Esau traded birthright for stew, illustrating danger of satisfying immediate appetite at eternal expense (Gen 25 :29-34). Demas deserted Paul, "loving this present world" (2 Tim 4 :10). Material gains can mask spiritual deficit until judgment reveals ledger. Jesus queries, "What will it profit a man if he gains the whole world and forfeits his soul?" (Matt 16 :26). Eternal bankruptcy is irreversible; gold becomes pavement, tears become gnashing. Wise stewards leverage possessions for kingdom investment, laying treasure where moth and rust cannot steal (Matt 6 :19-21). Assurance measured by heavenly account, not earthly portfolio, proves reliable.

4.6.4 Learning contentment beyond circumstantial favor Paul learned contentment in abundance and lack through strength of Christ (Phil 4 :11-13). Such equilibrium anchors assurance in God's unchanging character, not fluctuating assets. Spiritual disciplines like gratitude journaling, generosity, and fasting weaken material grip. Communities practicing shared burdens model alternative economy: believers distributing to anyone as need arises (Acts 4 :34-35). When wealth no longer defines identity, prosperity's allure fades, and trials no longer threaten self-worth. Contentment thus safeguards against false assurance by detaching salvation from circumstance.

4.7 Corporate Self-Deception in Churches and Movements

4.7.1 Triumph narrative: mistaking numbers for revival
David's census, driven by pride, brought plague (2 Sam 24 :1-10), warning leaders against equating headcounts with divine favor. Modern ministries tout attendance spikes as proof of Spirit, yet crowds can signal entertainment appeal rather than repentance. Jesus purposely thinned multitudes by preaching hard sayings (John 6 :60-66). Genuine revival exhibits deep conviction, restitution, hunger for doctrine. Metrics matter but must be weighed alongside fruit—holiness, missions, justice. Inflated triumph narratives foster complacency, obscuring need for ongoing reformation.

4.7.2 Echo chambers that drown prophetic rebuke
Ahab gathered four hundred prophets who echoed approval while Micaiah alone spoke doom (1 Kings 22 :6-14). Organizations may hire leaders who reinforce vision but silence critique, creating culture hostile to repentance. Social media algorithms amplify agreeable voices, entrenching groupthink. Healthy churches cultivate prophetic space where sin is named and power questioned. Elders welcome accountability, and laity practice Berean discernment (Acts 17 :11). Without such voices, corporate false assurance calcifies until judgment shatters illusion.

4.7.3 Institutional survival over gospel fidelity
Temple authorities plotted Jesus' death lest Romans remove place and nation (John 11 :48-50). Movements can prioritize brand protection, fund-raising, or political influence above doctrinal purity. When image management trumps truth, leaders downplay scandals, redefining sin to shield reputation. Christ, however, walks among lampstands and removes those that tolerate impurity (Rev 2 :5). Faithfulness may cost donors or status, yet better a small faithful remnant than a sprawling apostate empire. Corporate assurance must hinge on gospel fidelity, not institutional longevity.

4.7.4 Cultivating cultures of continual reformation The Reformation motto *semper reformanda*—"always being reformed"—applies to every era. Churches pursue regular self-examination through confessions, audits of justice, and openness to correction. Leadership plurality guards against autocracy, and external accountability networks provide perspective. Liturgy includes confession of corporate sins, reminding congregations they stand on grace. Such posture dismantles false assurance by acknowledging ongoing need for sanctifying truth. Communities thus stay nimble, ready to repent and align with Scripture whenever drift appears.

4.8 The Spirit's Alarms: Tests of Authentic Conversion

4.8.1 New affections for Christ and His commands (John 14 :15-23) Jesus links love for Him with obedience, promising manifest presence to such lovers. Regeneration rewires affections; commandments shift from burdens to delights. David cried, "Oh how I love Your law!" (Ps 119 :97), revealing heart surgery centuries before Pentecost. Evaluating assurance thus begins with appetite: Does the soul hunger for God's word, prayer, fellowship? Indifference signals danger, no matter prior profession. Love may fluctuate in warmth but persists in orientation, returning quickly when cooled. This relational magnetism distinguishes living faith from dead orthodoxy.

4.8.2 Ongoing repentance and war against sin (1 John 1 :6-10) John contrasts those who claim sinlessness with those who confess and receive cleansing. Genuine believers walk in light, where blemishes show, and bring them to Christ. Habitual patterns of hidden sin, excused or cherished, erode assurance. Battle itself, however, is evidence of life; corpses do not fight. Paul groaned over indwelling sin yet pressed forward (Rom 7 :24-25). Regular repentance, far from negating salvation, validates Spirit activity convicting and transforming. Assurance grows when gospel truth meets repeated failures with fresh grace empowering fresh obedience.

4.8.3 Love for the brethren and sacrificial service John states bluntly: whoever does not love his brother abides in death (1 John 3 :14). New birth implants family resemblance— affection for fellow believers across demographics. This love manifests tangibly: sharing goods, bearing burdens, forgiving offenses. Early Christians sold property to meet needs, stunning observers (Acts 2 :45). Lack of communal commitment—consumer church hopping, gossip, apathy toward suffering—raises red flags. Conversely, sacrificial service, even when unnoticed, reinforces inner witness of Spirit, assuring hearts before God (1 John 3 :18-19).

4.8.4 Perseverance amid trial as evidence of new life Jesus says only those who endure to the end will be saved (Matt 24 :13). Trials sift false professors like wind winnows chaff. Hebrews depicts true saints as those who shrink not back (Heb 10 :39). Perseverance is not stoic grit but Spirit-supplied faith that clings to promises through tears. Martyrs overcoming by Lamb's blood and testimony (Rev 12 :11) exemplify this grace. Observing steadfastness through illness, persecution, or obscurity strengthens both personal and corporate assurance, demonstrating reality of resurrection power.

4.9 Pastoral Strategies for Awakening the Self-Assured

4.9.1 Law-then-gospel preaching that wounds to heal The Puritans likened the law to a needle that precedes gospel thread; without puncture, thread cannot sew. Prophets and apostles expose sin relentlessly before unveiling pardon, following divine pattern at Sinai and Pentecost. Pastors must resist pressure to offer balm before lancing infection. Yet tone matters: wounds are dressed with tears, not scorn. When law convicts, gospel must flow immediately, lest despair crush hearers. Such preaching dismantles false assurance while securing true comfort in Christ.

4.9.2 Personal discipleship conversations marked by honest inquiry

Large gatherings rarely afford diagnostic depth; one-to-one discipleship allows probing questions about conversion story, hidden sins, spiritual disciplines. Jesus confronted Nicodemus privately, tailoring message to his misconception. Mentors listen, pray, and challenge assumptions gently, using scripture as mirror. Confidential spaces reduce performance pressure, enabling confession. Discipleship thus acts like spiritual MRI, revealing tumors unseen from pulpit. Faithful friends wound lovingly (Prov 27 :6), rescuing souls from self-deception.

4.9.3 Liturgical rhythms of confession and assurance

Weekly liturgies that move from adoration to confession to pardon train congregations to examine hearts regularly. Reading of law, corporate confession, and declaration of absolution reenact gospel drama. Over time, members distinguish between cheap and costly grace, learning to repent reflexively. Sacrament preparation—self-examination before Table—reinforces vigilance (1 Cor 11 :28). These rhythms embed spiritual cardiograms into worship, detecting arrhythmias early. False assurance suffocates in such environments; true assurance blossoms within honest dependence.

4.9.4 Community practices that expose and heal hypocrisy

Small groups that discuss sermons, share struggles, and pray cultivate transparency. Membership covenants set expectations for holiness and mutual exhortation. Church discipline, practiced graciously, warns wanderers and protects flock. Service projects reveal hearts— those seeking spotlight versus servants content unseen. When community life intersects daily realities—finances, parenting, anxiety—it surfaces inconsistencies and applies gospel remedies. Thus body life operates like immune system, identifying pathogens of hypocrisy and deploying antibodies of truth and love.

Conclusion

False assurance wears many disguises—ritual without regeneration, morality without mercy, doctrine without devotion, zeal without roots, prosperity without piety, and collective pride without prophetic scrutiny. Each costume flatters flesh while imperiling eternity. Scripture tears these garments, revealing naked souls in need of covering only Christ can provide. Yet exposure is mercy, not malice, for wounds revealed can be healed, and illusions shattered can give way to unshakeable joy. The wise will heed the Spirit's alarms, abandon sinking rafts of self-confidence, and cast themselves on the crucified Savior, whose blood secures pardon and whose Spirit seals perseverance. In that refuge assurance is neither flimsy presumption nor anxious uncertainty but settled peace that sings amid storms, knowing whom it has believed and persuaded He will keep what is entrusted to Him until that Day.

Chapter 5. The Awakening: Conviction by the Spirit

A spark in the soul can ignite a conflagration that rearranges an entire life. That spark is conviction—the Spirit-given realization that sin is not an unfortunate habit but high treason against the God who created, sustains, and judges. Conviction is not mere psychological discomfort, nor is it a preacher's manipulative leverage. It is the triune God's merciful first aid on a heart arrested by iniquity: a divine scalpel that cuts in order to heal. Without it the gravest warnings roll off the conscience like rain from polished marble; with it even whispered truth resounds like thunder. This chapter traces conviction's anatomy, instruments, stages, obstacles, evidences, historical eruptions, and pastoral stewardship. Each facet reveals a Spirit who is at once surgeon and counselor—wounding so He might bind, exposing that He may cover, unsettling in order to anchor. The goal is not to parade dramatic testimonies for voyeuristic effect but to help readers recognize, welcome, and cooperate with the Spirit's awakening work that alone can ferry them from false assurance to saving faith. May the following pages serve as lamp and mirror—lamp to illumine the Spirit's pathways, mirror to reflect our true condition—so that no one who reads remains drowsy on the precipice of eternal loss.

Prelude - When Sleeping Souls Begin to Stir

The "gentle gale of the Spirit" versus the "earthquake of conviction" Conviction can enter like a soft wind, hardly noticed at first, rustling a complacent soul with stray questions—*Why do I feel empty after success?*—or a seemingly casual scripture heard on the radio (1 Kings 19 :12). At other times it arrives as an earthquake, collapsing elaborate defenses in a single jolt when tragedy, betrayal, or a piercing sermon tears the veil (Acts 2 :37). Both modes are orchestrated by the same Spirit who hovers over chaos to birth new creation (Gen 1 :2). The gentle gale often begins with uneasiness over small compromises—an exaggeration here, a harsh word there—until cumulative weight presses conscience. The quake may blast through years of indifference, as Saul experienced on Damascus road when brilliant light and a rebuking voice flattened ambition (Acts 9 :3-6). Whether breeze or tremor, conviction disrupts self-reliance and opens eyes to God's holiness. Its diversity prevents prescriptive formulas; one sibling is wooed over months through quiet Bible readings, another is felled in a moment at a funeral. The Spirit tailors approach to temperament, history, and idols, yet the outcome aligns: sin grows bitter, Christ grows sweet. Believers must therefore avoid judging authenticity by intensity; depth is measured by ensuing repentance, not volcanic emotion. Recognizing multiple entryways into awakening guards against envy of dramatic stories and honors the Spirit's sovereign artistry.

Why conviction is a grace, not a cruelty To fallen minds, divine confrontation feels punitive, but scripture reclassifies it as loving discipline (Heb 12 :6-11). Like a physician palpating a hidden tumor, the Spirit's pressure hurts only because disease lurks beneath. If left untouched, sin metastasizes into eternal ruin; conviction arrests the spread. David's misery after his covert adultery was mercy hauling him back from abyss (Ps 32 :3-4). Jesus labels the Spirit "Paraclete"—

advocate—precisely when describing His convicting ministry (John 16 :8-11), teaching that prosecution and defense coincide in one divine Person: He indicts to secure acquittal through the cross. Cruelty would be silence that lets rebels stroll unwarned toward judgment. Grace raises alarms, sounding like thunder to sleepers but music to saints who recall their own awakening. Moreover, conviction safeguards communities: when Ananias and Sapphira fell, "great fear came upon all" (Acts 5 :11), purging duplicity and preserving purity. Thus, personal pain births communal health. Seeing conviction as grace shifts posture from dodging light to welcoming exposure, assured that the Surgeon carries balm with His blade.

Biblical snapshots of sudden awakening—from Isaiah's temple vision to Saul on Damascus Road Isaiah entered the temple perhaps expecting routine ritual but beheld seraphic glory, instantly crying, "Woe is me! I am undone" (Isa 6 :1-5). A righteous prophet discovered hidden filth when contrasted with thrice-holy radiance. Centuries later, Peter, overwhelmed by miraculous catch, fell at Jesus' knees: "Depart from me, for I am a sinful man" (Luke 5 :8). Conviction here erupted in vocational context—boats, nets—not sanctuary. The Philippian jailer, moments from suicide amid earthquake, begged, "What must I do to be saved?" (Acts 16 :27-30). His awakening blended cosmic tremor and apostolic compassion. These vignettes share common threads: encounter with divine holiness, acute self-awareness, and cry for mercy. They also display contextual variety—temple, lake, prison—underscoring the Spirit's omnipresent reach. Studying such awakenings builds expectancy: no workplace, prison cell, or pew is too ordinary for sudden illumination. They likewise warn seasoned believers that titles and tenure do not exempt one from fresh piercing; Isaiah had preached years before undone before glory. Thus biblical portraits become both invitation and mirror to modern readers.

5.1 The Nature of Spirit-Wrought Conviction

5.1.1 Conviction defined: divine light exposing hidden darkness (John 16 :8-11) Jesus promised the Spirit would "convict the world concerning sin, righteousness, and judgment." The Greek *elenchō* means to expose, convince, and refute, blending forensic and persuasive nuance. Conviction is therefore revelatory light flooding inner corridors where rationalization stored skeletons. It differs from generic guilt—often vague and self-centered—by pinpointing specific offenses against God's standard. It also contrasts with shame rooted in humiliation before people; true conviction focuses on divine audience (Ps 51 :4). Furthermore, it unveils righteousness, revealing Christ's perfection as both indictment—our deficiency—and hope—His sufficiency. Finally, it certifies judgment: the cross and empty tomb prove that refusal to believe places one under already-issued sentence. Thus conviction is multidimensional illumination orienting sinner to reality: self unmasked, Christ revealed, destiny clarified. Anything less—mere sorrow for consequences or fear of exposure—falls short of Spirit-wrought awakening.

5.1.2 Distinguishing true conviction from vague guilt or human shame Vague guilt loiters without direction—an overcast mood absent clear sin identified. It often springs from personality bent toward scrupulosity or from legalistic cultures measuring worth by performance. Human shame focuses on reputation, fretting, "What will they think?" after indiscretion. Spirit conviction, by contrast, names evil in God-referencing terms and escorts the conscience toward remedy. David's confession, "Against You only have I sinned" (Ps 51 :4), illustrates vertical orientation even while acknowledging horizontal damage. Another hallmark is hope: though pierced, the soul senses provision beckoning, whereas worldly sorrow breeds despair (2 Cor 7 :10). Finally, true conviction produces lasting transformation, not cyclical penance; it implants hatred for sin and love for obedience. Discerning these differences spares believers from Satan's counterfeit either of crushing accusation (Rev 12 :10) or superficial remorse that never repents.

5.1.3 Holiness revealed, self unmasked: the two-fold axis of awakening Isaiah's cry fused upward vision and inward collapse; only when eyes beheld King did lips cry unclean. Conviction therefore pivots on twin revelations: God's blazing purity and one's polluted heart. If holiness is dim, sin seems minor; if sin is minimized, grace is cheap. The Spirit elevates both poles simultaneously, increasing contrast until pride yields. At Sinai lightning and smoke framed Ten Commandments, and people begged distance (Ex 20 :18-19). Peter, glimpsing resurrected authority, wept bitterly (Luke 22 :61-62). Such encounters fuel authentic worship because adoration rises from humbled awe, not flattery. Churches that showcase divine attributes—sovereignty, justice, majesty—become fertile soil for conviction, whereas sentimental depictions domesticate God and blunt awakenings. Thus preaching must paint holiness vivid before prescribing application.

5.1.4 Tears, terror, or quiet clarity—varied emotional textures of the same work Some experience conviction as torrents of tears, collapsing at altars; others lie awake restrained by solemn dread; still others register quiet certainty that they are lost. Emotion varies with temperament, upbringing, and circumstances, but essence remains Spirit disclosure. Nicodemus conversed civilly with Jesus yet left pondering new birth (John 3). Conversely, the crowds at Pentecost were "cut to the heart" en masse (Acts 2 :37). Recognizing emotional diversity prevents judgment: the stoic may be deeply convicted though dry-eyed, the expressive may weep without lasting change. Pastors must affirm content of conviction—confession of sin, desire for Christ—over dramatic display. Individuals should avoid chasing feelings and instead examine fruit: does sin taste bitter, does obedience beckon? The Spirit personalizes conviction's hue but standardizes its trajectory toward repentance and faith.

5.2 Primary Instruments the Spirit Employs

5.2.1 The preached Word: hammer, mirror, and seed (Jer 23 :29; Jas 1 :22-25) God's Word shatters rock-hard hearts like a hammer, reveals motives like a mirror, and germinates life like a seed. During Peter's Pentecost sermon, scripture-filled proclamation pierced thousands (Acts 2 :14-36). The Spirit authored scripture; thus He wields it with surgical precision, applying ancient text to contemporary conscience. Expository preaching positions hearers under this anvil, trusting impact to divine agency rather than rhetorical flair. Yet casual Bible reading can convict too: Augustine heard "take and read," opened Romans, and chains fell. Because Word never returns void (Isa 55 :10-11), even tracts left in laundromats can ignite awakening. Believers should saturate conversations with scripture, not clichés, for verses carry Spirit potency. Confidence in Word breeds boldness and patience, knowing that sometimes seed germinates underground long before shoots appear.

5.2.2 Providence: crisis and calamity as wakeners of conscience Famine drove prodigal to himself; storm drove Jonah to confession; plague humbled Pharaoh's magicians. Providential hardships dismantle self-sufficiency, making ears attentive to divine whisper. C. S. Lewis called pain "God's megaphone to rouse a deaf world." Yet prosperity can also convict when emptiness surfaces amid plenty, as Solomon discovered (Eccl 2 :11). The Spirit orchestrates external events—job loss, diagnosis, promotion—to expose internal void. Interpreting providence requires scripture lens; calamity alone may embitter unless guided to redemption. Christians walking with suffering neighbors must resist trite answers, instead tracing threads from broken cisterns to living water (Jer 2 :13). Thus, providence is raw material; the Spirit sculpts conviction through it, inviting surrender rather than resentment.

5.2.3 Conscience: the Spirit's courtroom in the inner man (Rom 2 :14-15) Conscience functions like a skylight admitting moral light, though grime of sin dims it. The Spirit cleanses pane to restore clarity, accusing or excusing thoughts. When David secretly cut Saul's robe, "his heart struck him" (1 Sam 24 :5); no prophet needed. Unchecked, conscience can be seared, losing sensitivity (1 Tim 4 :2). The Spirit re-sensitizes by comparing behavior with law, pricking even socially acceptable sins like envy or indifference. Because conscience operates continuously, conviction via this avenue may feel like persistent disquiet rather than sermon thunder. Responding quickly keeps heart soft; repeated suppression stiffens it. Believers pray with Psalmist, "Search me...see if any grievous way" (Ps 139 :23-24), inviting Spirit audit.

5.2.4 Christian community: testimony, discipline, and holy contagion Iron sharpens iron; so fellowship sparks conviction through stories of grace, mutual admonition, and observed holiness. Nathan's parable confronted David within relational trust, shattering royal denial (2 Sam 12 :1-13). Church discipline in Corinth aimed to awaken immoral brother by social exclusion (1 Cor 5 :4-5). Positive contagion occurs when new converts' zeal exposes veterans' complacency, or sacrificial generosity rebukes materialism. Corporate worship amplifies Word and Spirit as voices harmonize in confession and praise. Isolation dulls conviction; community fans it. Thus believers must resist consumer Christianity and embed in accountable relationships where blind spots are lovingly illuminated.

5.3 Progressive Stages of Awakening

5.3.1 Illumination of mind: realizing objective guilt Conviction often begins intellectually: doctrines once abstract connect personally. Peter's sermon linked crucifixion to listeners: "this Jesus whom *you* crucified" (Acts 2 :36). God's commands, previously external, become verdicts against self. Legal metaphors—debt, verdict, wages—clarify status, refuting self-righteous narratives. Mind illumination doesn't save but sets stage; awareness without remedy could engender despair or resistance. Nevertheless it is essential, for faith involves understanding (Rom 10 :14-17). Catechesis enhances this phase, providing categories—holiness, wrath, substitution—by which Spirit convicts. Conversely, doctrinal ignorance may blunt awakening, leaving vague discomfort unchanneled. Thus churches must teach law clearly so Spirit can wield it sharply.

5.3.2 Piercing of affections: sorrow according to God (2 Cor 7 :9-10)
Knowledge soon rouses emotion—shame, grief, fear—when heart feels weight of guilt. Godly sorrow differs from self-pity; it weeps over having offended God, not merely over consequences. Peter's bitter tears post-denial reveal affection wound (Luke 22 :62). This stage may involve physical manifestations—sob, tremor—but inward posture matters: humility. Some cultures suppress emotion; Spirit may still pierce quietly, but appetite changes—laughter rings hollow, hobbies lose luster. Such sorrow is productive, leading to diligence and zeal, unlike worldly remorse that breeds paralyzing regret. Pastors must tenderly shepherd here, assuring that tears are seeds of joy when watered by gospel.

5.3.3 Trembling of will: the crisis of surrender (Acts 16 :29-30)
Intellect awakened, heart pierced, the will now stands at crossroads: retain sovereignty or capitulate. The jailer fell trembling, asking for salvation—an act of volitional surrender. Resistance often peaks here; pride marshals arguments, habits clamor. Spirit applies pressure through continued discomfort, vivid dreams, or repeated messages. Once will bows, words flow—"Lord, what do You want?"—signaling shift from rebellion to submission. Yet surrender is not meritorious work; it is evacuation of self-trust, embracing alien righteousness. Counselors should clarify gospel, lest seeker attempt to barter promises of reform. True surrender receives before it resolves, drawing strength for future obedience from present union.

5.3.4 Dawning of hope: glimpses of Christ as sufficient refuge
Conviction is incomplete without gospel dawn. Like morning light after a stormy night, hope breaks when soul beholds crucified-risen Savior adequate for deepest stain. Isaiah's coal cleansed once-condemned lips (Isa 6 :6-7); jailer rejoiced with household before dawn (Acts 16 :34). Hope

emerges as Spirit testifies of Christ's sufficiency, perhaps through hymn line—"My sin, not in part but the whole"—or verse—"whoever comes I will never cast out" (John 6 :37). Weight lifts, replaced by peace surpassing understanding. Important: hope arises not from self-analysis of sincerity but from gazing at finished work. This assurance propels repentance and faith detailed next chapter. Thus awakening culminates in paradox: broken yet mended, guilty yet justified, trembling yet rejoicing.

5.4 Common Obstacles and Quenchers

5.4.1 Procrastination and the myth of "a more convenient season" (Acts 24 :25) Felix trembled under Paul's discourse but deferred decision, clinging to power and bribes. Delay dulls conviction; initial pangs fade like muscle aches ignored. Satan whispers, "Tomorrow," turning moments of clarity into memories of discomfort. Heart calcification follows, for repeated refusal sears conscience (Heb 3 :13). Scripture counters with urgency: "Today if you hear His voice…" (Ps 95 :7-8). Evangelists must press hearers lovingly, explaining life's vapor (Jas 4 :14). Believers should promptly obey smaller convictions to cultivate responsiveness, lest procrastination morph into pattern. Redeeming time includes seizing conviction's window before shutters close.

5.4.2 Rationalization: intellectual smokescreens against moral light Unbelievers erect arguments—textual criticism, hypocrite charges—to divert from sin issue. Reasoned dialogue is vital, but often questions mask heart unwillingness. Jesus answered Sadducees' resurrection riddle yet denounced ignorance of power (Matt 22 :29). Apologists must discern genuine seekers and smoke-screeners, steering debate to Christ's claims. Believers likewise rationalize—"I'm not as bad as…"—to silence Spirit. Scripture dismantles excuses: all have sinned (Rom 3 :23). Honest confession drives fog away; clinging to rationalization quenches Spirit by elevating intellect above revelation.

5.4.3 Peer pressure and cultural anesthetics Fear of family ridicule or professional loss muzzles awakened souls. John notes rulers who believed but hid faith lest expelled from synagogue (John 12 :42-43). Culture supplies anesthetics—entertainment, substance, busyness—to drown convicting voice. Daniel's peers faced furnace yet stood; their courage indicts compromise (Dan 3). Churches can combat peer pressure by providing supportive fellowship where confession meets grace. Practices like digital Sabbath counter anesthetics, creating silence where Spirit speaks. Ultimate remedy is fear of God exceeding fear of men (Matt 10 :28).

5.4.4 Satanic counter-conviction: false comfort, false despair Enemy mirrors Spirit's work in two distortions: minimizing sin or magnifying it beyond pardon. False comfort whispers, "Peace, peace" when none (Jer 6 :14), urging morality tweaks rather than surrender. False despair insists sin too vile for cross, like Judas' remorse without return. Both quench genuine conviction by diverting from Christ. Ephesians 6 exhorts putting on truth belt and faith shield to extinguish fiery darts. Saints combat lies with gospel promises: "Though your sins are scarlet..." (Isa 1 :18). Community prayer and scripture memorization fortify minds against diabolical distortions.

5.5 Fruit That Confirms Genuine Conviction

5.5.1 Confession without excuses (Psalm 32 :5) David modelled transparent acknowledgment: "I said, I will confess... and You forgave." No blame shifted to Bathsheba's beauty or palace stress. Genuine conviction produces similar candor—naming sins, not circumstances. In revival narratives, public confessions detail thefts, lies, secret grudges, prompting restitution. Such vulnerability evidences Spirit, for flesh seeks image preservation. Yet confession aims at God's glory, not exhibitionism; details serve to magnify grace, not gratify morbid curiosity. Privacy principles apply. Ultimately, confession's sincerity seen in forsaking sin (Prov 28 :13).

Continual acknowledgement forms lifestyle of humble dependence rather than one-time catharsis.

5.5.2 Hatred of sin coupled with hunger for holiness Conviction changes taste buds: once-sweet habits become bitter, righteousness attractive. Paul, formerly proud of pedigree, counted all loss for Christ (Phil 3 :7-8). New appetite shows in drastic measures—cutting off stumbling hands (Mark 9 :43-47)—not to earn salvation but to enjoy it. Sin lingers, but attitude shifts from pet to pest. Prayers pivot: "Lord, expose hidden faults; lead me in way everlasting" (Ps 139 :24). This holy antipathy fuels vigilance, accountability, and reliance on means of grace. Absence of sin-hatred signals superficial conviction; presence of both aversion and attraction confirms Spirit renovation.

5.5.3 Restitution and reconciliation where possible (Luke 19 :8-9) Zacchaeus demonstrated inward change by outward reparations—fourfold to defrauded. Conviction prompts tangible steps: returning stolen money, confessing slander, apologizing to estranged relatives, dismantling unethical business practices. While not always feasible or prerequisite for forgiveness, restitution expresses repentance's sincerity and heals wounds. Mosaic law prescribed compensation to victims, reflecting God's justice (Ex 22 :1-5). Modern application might involve academic plagiarism confession, crediting original sources publicly. Such actions often open evangelistic doors as victims witness gospel power. Avoiding restitution when possible may reveal lingering pride; seeking it showcases Spirit fruit.

5.5.4 Persistent seeking of Christ rather than fleeting emotion Post-awakening, convicted souls press into prayer, scripture, fellowship, refusing to rest until assurance dawns. Syrophoenician woman persisted despite initial silence, obtaining deliverance (Mark 7 :25-30). This pursuit distinguishes genuine conviction from momentary scare; once emotional wave subsides, hunger endures. Early Methodists required "society tickets" where seekers met for accountability until witnessing pardon. Today, involvement in discipleship groups, baptism classes, service teams indicates pursuit.

Conversely, disappearing after altar call suggests seed snatched by birds. The Spirit who convicts also draws toward Christ; following that pull evidences authenticity.

5.6 Historical and Contemporary Revivals as Case Studies

5.6.1 The First Great Awakening: Edwards, Whitefield, and the "surprising work" In 1730s-40s New England, ordinary parishioners experienced profound conviction under plain preaching. Edwards described listeners groaning aloud, clinging to pews, fearing hell. Yet emotional phenomena accompanied doctrinal clarity; sermons expounded justification by faith. George Whitefield's itinerant oratory drew tens of thousands, but he insisted conversion evidenced by holy living, thus channeling conviction toward discipleship. Opponents decried enthusiasm, yet societal reforms—abolition seeds, missions surge—followed. The revival illustrates mass conviction igniting when Word and Spirit converge, challenging complacent religiosity.

5.6.2 The 1857–58 Prayer Revival and the anatomy of lay conviction Jeremiah Lanphier's noon prayer in New York started with six attendees; within months, thousands gathered daily, confessing sin and seeking mercy. No celebrity preacher led; Spirit conviction spread through testimonies and simple Bible reading. Estimates record one million converts across America. Economic panic had softened hearts, showing providence preparing soil. Conviction here manifested in quiet weeping, business closures for prayer, and reconciliation between labor and management. The movement underscores prayer's role as bell inviting Spirit to ring conviction across social strata.

5.6.3 Welsh and Korean awakenings: national tremors of repentance In 1904-05 Wales, Evan Roberts urged, "Bend me," and coal miners wept, returning stolen tools, taming pit ponies confused by absence of profanity. Bars emptied, police idled, hymn-singing filled streets. Similarly, Korea's 1907

Pyongyang Revival began with elders publicly confessing grudges, unleashing widespread repentance that birthed missionary movement. Both awakenings featured corporate conviction leading to societal transformation—crime reduction, reconciliation across classes, surge in church planting. They caution against individualistic frameworks: Spirit often convicts communities, not just persons.

5.6.4 Lessons for modern churches longing for fresh visitation Historical revivals share patterns: fervent prayer, fearless preaching, holiness hunger, humble leadership, social impact. Yet attempts to manufacture phenomena fail; conviction is sovereignty, not strategy. Churches can till soil—teach doctrine, prioritize repentance liturgies, foster unity, plead in prayer—but cannot coerce rain. They must also prepare nets: discipleship systems to mature converts lest shallow soil syndrome squander harvest. Revival may disrupt schedules, budgets, reputations; leaders must value Spirit agenda above comfort. Most importantly, conviction cannot remain nostalgic memory; its legacy must shape present longing for God's glory in fresh generations.

5.7 Pastoral and Missional Implications

5.7.1 Cultivating an atmosphere hospitable to conviction—prayer, truth, authenticity Pastors serve as spiritual meteorologists, removing umbrellas of distraction so Spirit rain may fall. Corporate prayer signals dependence; truth-rich sermons pierce; authenticity from pulpit models repentance. If leaders confess sins publicly, congregants feel safe to own theirs. Entertainment-driven services anesthetize; reverent worship awakens. Space for silence allows Spirit whisper; liturgies of lament legitimize brokenness. Hospitality ministries create entry points for seekers wrestling conviction without church vocabulary. Thus environment matters: while Spirit is sovereign, He often chooses vessels prepared in humility.

5.7.2 Counseling the newly awakened: guiding sorrow toward gospel rest Awakened individuals may oscillate between hope and fear. Counselors should listen, clarify gospel, dispel misconceptions, and avoid pushing premature assurance or dampening godly sorrow. Use scripture like 1 John 1 :9, Isaiah 55 :7, showing abundant pardon. Encourage habits—daily Word, prayer, fellowship—to nurture tender shoot. Address practical restitution steps. Monitor for legalistic self-atonement tendencies; redirect to Christ's sufficiency. Offer baptism instruction as tangible embrace of grace. Such guidance shepherds conviction into conversion, preventing emotional fizz or despair.

5.7.3 Guarding against manipulation while pleading earnestly Some equate conviction with volume or gimmicks— dim lights, extended music, fear-mongering stories. Manipulation produces spurious responses and eventual cynicism. Paul refused cunning but set forth truth plainly (2 Cor 4 :2). Yet earnest pleading is biblical; Christ wept over Jerusalem. Balance lies in vivid exposition of law and gospel, prayerful dependence, and invitation anchored in scripture. Observers should attribute awakening to Spirit, not human technique, safeguarding God's glory and converts' stability.

5.7.4 Channeling awakened hearts into disciple-making mission Freshly convicted believers possess zeal that can stall without direction. Early church channeled new converts into apostolic teaching, fellowship, sacraments, and mission (Acts 2 :42-47). Ministries should mobilize them—evangelism teams, mercy projects—so outward flow sustains inward fire. Mentoring pairs maturity with zeal. Mission participation reinforces grace: sharing gospel reminds newly awakened of their deliverance, deepening assurance. Thus conviction's ripple expands beyond individual to nations, fulfilling Spirit's Pentecost purpose.

Conclusion

Conviction is the Spirit's holy siege, laying bare sin's fortress so that gates may open to the conquering grace of Christ. He employs Word, providence, conscience, and community to illuminate mind, pierce affections, and bend will, overcoming procrastination, rationalization, peer pressure, and demonic counterfeits. Authentic conviction bears fruit—honest confession, sin-hatred, restitution, persevering pursuit of Jesus—validated across history in awakenings that re-formed societies and propelled missions. Pastors and congregations are called to host this grace through prayer-soaked truth and humble authenticity, avoiding manipulation while pleading earnestly. Yet conviction is not terminus: it must flow into repentance, faith, and Spirit-empowered discipleship that multiplies awakening in others. May every reader heed the still small voice or the thunderous quake, refusing false comfort, embracing the wound that heals, and joining the long procession of saints who once cried out, "What must I do to be saved?" and now proclaim, "To Him who loves us and has freed us from our sins by His blood... be glory and dominion forever and ever" (Rev 1 :5-6).

Chapter 6. The Gift and Demand of Repentance

Repentance is the hinge on which the great door of salvation swings. It is the Spirit-empowered about-face that carries a sinner from clinging self-love toward surrendered God-love, from treasuring idols toward treasuring Christ. Because conviction (Chapter 5) illumines sin and awakens need, repentance now supplies the decisive pivot from awakened grief to life-giving obedience. Scripture consistently presents this turn as both a gracious gift—"God has granted repentance that leads to life" (Acts 11 :18)—and an urgent command— "God now commands all people everywhere to repent" (Acts 17 :30). The pages that follow explore that paradox. They trace repentance through biblical epochs, dissect its anatomy, expose counterfeits, and display the fruit that inevitably blossoms when hearts truly turn. Pastoral counsel and eschatological urgency frame the discussion, showing why repentance is not merely an initiation rite but a lifelong rhythm of the gospel. The prayer undergirding every sentence is that readers, hearing the Spirit's call, will experience the joy that overflows whenever even one sinner turns and heaven erupts in celebration.

Prelude - Turning at the Crossroads

Repentance in one sentence: a God-given U-turn of mind, heart, and life When Scripture employs the Greek *metanoia* and the Hebrew *shuv*, it captures the image of travellers reversing course after realizing every step carried them deeper into danger. Repentance therefore involves intellectual recognition—confessing that the path of sin violates God's law; emotional agreement—feeling grief for having spurned divine love; and volitional action—walking in an entirely new direction. This U-turn is not self-improvement but Spirit-infused reorientation: the mind is renewed (Rom 12 :2), the heart of stone becomes flesh (Ezek 36 :26), and the feet learn new habits of righteousness (Col 1 :10). Because the Spirit supplies illumination, sorrow, and power, humans cannot boast. Yet the call to turn is addressed to human faculties—to think, to feel, to choose—so responsibility remains. Whenever gospel heralds cry, "Repent and believe" (Mark 1 :15), they summon rebels to receive a gift that, paradoxically, must also be obeyed. Every genuine conversion story, regardless of culture or background, features that God-given U-turn at its center.

Why the call to repent is mercy, not moralism (Rom 2 :4) Some recoil at the word *repent*, imagining finger-wagging legalists. Paul demolishes that caricature when he attributes repentance to "the riches of [God's] kindness." Divine patience extends the timeline; kindness exposes idols gently; forbearance stays judgment long enough for prodigals to come home. Were God indifferent, He would let sinners sprint toward destruction unopposed. Instead, like a shepherd leaving ninety-nine to pursue one, He interrupts wandering with a corrective crook. The imperative "Repent!" is therefore more akin to a lifeguard's "Grab the rope!" than to a drill sergeant's bark. It is moral, because it demands ethical about-face, but never moralistic, because its motive is love, its means is grace, and its end is joy. Failing to preach repentance with tenderness misrepresents God; refusing to heed the call scorns the very kindness that might have led to life.

Metanoia through the ages—from Noah's world to the message of the apostles Noah's generation heard a century-long sermon hammered into ark timbers, yet only eight souls repented (1 Pet 3 :20). Nineveh, by contrast, donned sackcloth from throne to cattle at Jonah's reluctant warning, and judgment was postponed (Jon 3 :5-10). Prophets repeatedly pled with Judah to turn, promising healing (Jer 3 :22) and restoration (Hos 14 :1-4). When John the Baptist thundered in the wilderness, he stood in that prophetic stream, preparing hearts for Messiah by baptizing repentant crowds (Matt 3 :2-8). Jesus began His public preaching with the identical cry—"Repent, for the kingdom of heaven is at hand" (Matt 4 :17)—then commissioned apostles to proclaim "repentance for the forgiveness of sins" to all nations (Luke 24 :47). Church history perpetuates the call: Luther's first thesis declared that all of life is repentance; revivals from Wales to Korea have always featured weeping and turning before singing and sending. Thus, metanoia is the constant thread stitching together the redemptive tapestry from floodwaters to future glory.

6.1 Repentance in the Grammar of the Gospel

6.1.1 Two sides of one coin: repentance and faith inseparable (Mark 1 :15) Jesus' inaugural summary of the gospel places "repent" and "believe" side by side, joined like the two inseparable faces of a single coin. Repentance is the negative turn from sin; faith is the positive turn toward Christ. Remove either and the gospel collapses: a sinner who tries to forsake sin without trusting the Savior merely swaps vices or becomes self-righteous, while a person who professes belief without abandoning idols proves his faith dead (Jas 2 :17). Acts 20 :21 captures apostolic cadence—"repentance toward God and faith in our Lord Jesus Christ"—indicating direction (toward God) and object (Jesus) for the turning heart. Pastors must therefore avoid preaching "believe" in isolation, lest hearers assume intellectual assent suffices, and must avoid preaching "repent" as moral reform without offering Christ's righteousness. Both motions occur in the same Spirit-wrought heartbeat, though awareness of each may unfold progressively. This grammatical unity safeguards the gospel from antinomian laxity and legalistic rigor alike.

6.1.2 The Trinitarian logic—Father's kindness, Spirit's conviction, Son's atoning ground The whole Trinity orchestrates repentance. The Father initiates kindness (Rom 2 :4) and grants repentance (Acts 5 :31), the Son purchases legal grounds by bearing curse (Gal 3 :13), and the Spirit applies conviction (John 16 :8). Without Calvary, turning could not secure pardon; without the Spirit, blindness would persist; without the Father's design, neither cross nor conviction would exist. Thus repentance magnifies Trinitarian harmony: each Person distinct yet united in rescuing rebels. Believers responding to this grace find themselves drawn not merely into legal acquittal but into familial embrace—Spirit of adoption teaches them to cry, "Abba !" (Rom 8 :15). Preaching must therefore celebrate, not sever, this triune choreography, anchoring repentance in relational love rather than abstract ethics.

6.1.3 Gift or command?—holding divine enablement and human responsibility in tension Peter declares that God "granted" repentance to the Gentiles (Acts 11 :18), yet also commands all people to repent (Acts 17 :30). This tension mirrors salvation itself: God sovereignly regenerates, humans freely believe. Repentance as gift humbles, preventing pride in one's turning; repentance as command warns against fatalism and excuses. Philippians 2 :12-13 captures balance— work out salvation because God works within. When a sinner heeds the call, heaven credits God's grace; when a sinner refuses, scripture lays blame squarely on stubbornness. Pastors must resist simplistic resolutions (e.g., repentance depends entirely on free will or is unnecessary because predestined) and instead let both truths produce urgency and humility.

6.1.4 False dichotomies to avoid: penance vs. grace, sorrow vs. joy
Medieval theology often equated repentance with acts of penance—pilgrimages, flagellations—to earn forgiveness. Reformers rightly recovered grace, yet modern swings can so emphasize gratuity that sorrow is downplayed. Biblical repentance contains both: profound grief at offending love and exuberant joy at receiving mercy (Ps 30 :11-12). Likewise, tears do not contradict assurance; they prepare soil for gladness. Elijah's fire fell after water-drenched sacrifice; so gospel fire falls where contrition soaks pride. Healthy teaching avoids pitting sorrow against joy or transformation against acceptance. Instead, it portrays the sequence: grace produces brokenness which blossoms into glad obedience, ensuring repentance remains sweet even when it stings.

6.2 Old-Testament Roots of a New-Covenant Reality

6.2.1 Shuv: the Hebrew turn—prophetic summons to covenant faithfulness
The dominant Old-Testament verb for repent, *shuv*, literally means to return. Prophets employ it over a thousand times, pleading for Israel to come back to Yahweh after wandering. Jeremiah 3 :22 captures divine heart: "Return, O faithless children, I will heal your faithlessness." The relational nuance distinguishes biblical repentance from rote regret; it is homecoming, not merely behavior modification. Because Israel's covenant framed obedience as love response, turning always involved relational reconciliation—breaking idols, rebuilding altars, renewing vows. Thus, *shuv* lays groundwork for New-Testament metanoia: gospel calls sinners not just to different morals but to restored fellowship with God.

6.2.2 Sackcloth, ashes, and solemn assemblies: symbolic pedagogy of contrition
Ancient Near Eastern cultures expressed grief with visible symbols—torn garments, dust-covered heads. Israel harnessed these for communal repentance: Joel commands elders to "call a solemn assembly...cry out to the Lord" (Joel 1 :13-14). Such rituals

embodied inward sorrow, teaching generations the gravity of sin. Yet prophets insisted symbolism without heart change was abomination (Isa 58 :5-7). Therefore, sackcloth served as catechism, not magic—external sign pointing to internal posture. Modern equivalents might include corporate fasting or public testimonies of confession. Physical acts, rightly employed, can reinforce repentance by engaging body in soul's turn, reminding worshipers that grace concerns whole person.

6.2.3 National repentance in Nineveh and Judah: collective pivots from impending wrath (Jon 3; 2 Chr 34)

When Jonah begrudgingly preached, Nineveh's king led nation-wide fast, even animals robed in sackcloth, and God relented. Remarkably, pagan city out-repented covenant people, shaming Israel's stubbornness and foreshadowing Gentile inclusion. Under Josiah, Judah rediscovered law, smashed idols, renewed Passover, and postponed exile (2 Kings 22-23). These episodes reveal that repentance can be corporate, influencing divine dealings with societies. Contemporary communities—churches, cities, nations— should not dismiss collective guilt. Racial injustices, systemic greed, ecological abuse call for multi-voice lament and reform. While salvation is personal, repentance may be social, demonstrating kingdom righteousness in public ethics.

6.2.4 Promised heart-circumcision: Deuteronomy's future hope (Deut 30 :1-6)

Moses, foreseeing Israel's inevitable exile, predicted a time when God would circumcise hearts so that people could truly love Him. This proto-promise anticipates Jeremiah's new covenant and Ezekiel's Spirit infusion (Jer 31 :31-34; Ezek 36 :26-27). True repentance, therefore, awaited regenerative heart surgery accomplished at Pentecost. Old-Testament saints experienced genuine turns, but the widespread, durable obedience envisioned required inner transformation. Christians today live in fulfilment of that hope: repentance is not self-generated but Spirit-enabled, fulfilling Deuteronomy's prophetic vision. Understanding this continuity enriches gratitude and frames repentance as participation in long-promised renewal.

6.3 The Anatomy of Genuine Repentance

6.3.1 Intellectual recognition: agreeing with God's verdict on sin Repentance begins when the mind capitulates to divine evaluation: "I have sinned against the LORD" (2 Sam 12 :13). This acknowledgment transcends general imperfection; it names specific transgressions—lust, envy, deceit—and confesses their offensiveness. It also affirms God's right to judge—"so that You may be justified in Your words" (Ps 51 :4). Such intellectual shift uproots excuses, comparisons, and blame. Catechesis aids this process by defining sin not merely as personal injury but as violation of God's holy law. When minds embrace that verdict, defensive rationalizations collapse, making space for deeper heart work. Failure at this step spawns superficial repentance—tears over consequences but clinging to self-justification. Thus pastors must teach law clearly to illuminate sin's seriousness before prescribing grace.

6.3.2 Emotional brokenness: godly sorrow distinguished from self-pity (2 Cor 7 :9-11) Paul celebrates Corinth's grief because it was "according to God," producing earnestness and zeal. Godly sorrow aches primarily for how sin dishonors God and wounds others; worldly sorrow moans over lost ease or exposed reputation. The tax collector's plea, "God, be merciful to me, a sinner" (Luke 18 :13), embodies true contrition—no alibis, only dependence. This emotional response is God's gift; it cannot be manufactured yet should be cultivated through meditation on cross and law. While temperament affects expression—some sob, others become contemplatively heavy—all genuine brokenness moves the heart from rebellion to receptivity. Self-pity, however, curves inward, leading to despair or anger; it shrinks under correction and often blames circumstances. Therefore counselors discern sorrow's flavor: does it breed humility and eagerness for restitution, or depression and self-absorption? Only the former signals authentic repentance.

6.3.3 Volitional reorientation: decisive renunciation and new allegiance The prodigal not only lamented pig-sty hunger but resolved, "I will arise and go to my father" (Luke

15 :18). Repentance crystallizes in choices: ending adulterous relationship, deleting shady apps, confessing fraud to employer, scheduling baptism. These decisions flow from new allegiance—Jesus is Lord. Volitional turn may involve painful cost; Zacchaeus parted with half his possessions. Grace supplies strength, yet disciples must calculate and embrace cross (Luke 14 :27-33). Half-measures reveal lingering idolatry. Nevertheless, volitional reorientation is not perfection but direction; a stumble does not nullify repentance if trajectory remains God-ward. Thus spiritual mentors balance high call with patient encouragement, celebrating steps while urging full surrender.

6.3.4 Ongoing posture: repentance as daily lifestyle, not a one-time event Martin Luther's first Ninety-five Thesis insists that Christ willed "the entire life of believers to be one of repentance." Conversion inaugurates rhythm: quick confession, swift return, fresh obedience. 1 John 1 :9 invites continual cleansing; Lord's Prayer includes daily plea for forgiveness. Progressive sanctification depends on recurring micro-turns—renouncing new idols, updating motives, recalibrating trust. Unlike morbid introspection, daily repentance liberates joy by offloading sin's accruing weight. Marriage and community thrive when members repent often, preventing bitter roots. Heaven will end tears, but until then believers breathe repentance in and gospel assurance out, like spiritual respiration sustaining life.

6.4 Counterfeits and Short-Circuits

6.4.1 Worldly regret: Esau's tears and Judas' despair Hebrews 12 :17 cites Esau, who sought blessing with tears yet found no place for repentance; his sorrow mourned lost blessing, not offended God. Judas, remorseful after betrayal, returned blood money but hanged himself (Matt 27 :3-5), illustrating despair devoid of faith. Both examples warn that emotion alone cannot save. Worldly regret fixates on consequences—reputation ruined, comforts forfeited—while heart idols remain enthroned. It often produces self-harm or cynical cynicism. Pastoral discernment must detect this counterfeit, steering mourners beyond consequences to God-centered confession and faith. Gospel hope can rescue despairing hearts, but only when they reorient toward Christ rather than inward misery.

6.4.2 Mechanical penance: rituals that soothe conscience but dodge surrender Religious impulse often seeks tangible acts—alms, pilgrimages, volunteerism—to offset guilt. Israel offered sacrifices while plotting evil, prompting divine disgust: "I cannot endure iniquity and solemn assembly" (Isa 1 :13). Modern equivalents include lengthy devotions performed without contrite heart or social activism substituting for personal holiness. These mechanical penances inoculate conscience, providing illusion of repentance without true change. Salvation cannot be bought; sacrifice God accepts is broken spirit (Ps 51 :17). Thus preaching must dismantle barter mentality, presenting Christ's once-for-all sacrifice as sole atonement and obedience as gratitude response, not appeasement currency.

6.4.3 Selective repentance: editing sin list to preserve cherished idols King Herod revered John the Baptist, did many things, yet refused to relinquish Herodias (Mark 6 :20). Selective repentance negotiates, surrendering visible vices while guarding secret ones—perhaps pornography, bitterness, pride. Like Saul sparing Agag, it keeps attractive spoils (1 Sam 15 :9). God calls for whole-hearted turning; partial obedience equates rebellion. James warns that violating one point of law makes one guilty of all (Jas 2 :10). Sanctification may progress incrementally, but willful retention of known sin invalidates repentance. Discipleship relationships help expose hidden idols, fostering holistic turn. Selective repentance is thus a mirage—appearing penitent while remaining enslaved.

6.4.4 Hyper-grace denial of the demand: antinomian blind spots then and now (Jude 4) Jude confronted teachers who perverted grace into license, denying that believers must forsake sin. Modern hyper-grace narratives insist repentance simply means changing one's mind about being righteous already, eliminating sorrow and confession. Such teaching neuters New-Testament imperatives calling believers to "put to death" sinful deeds (Col 3 :5). Grace indeed pardons fully, but Titus 2 :12 says it also trains to renounce ungodliness. Any gospel devoid of repentance falls under Paul's "let him be accursed" (Gal 1 :8). Pastors combating antinomianism must portray grace in full color: costly blood bought freedom *from* sin's rule, not freedom *to* indulge. True assurance blossoms not by ignoring sin but by watching Christ conquer it within.

6.5 Fruits Worthy of Repentance

6.5.1 Inner realignment: new affections, reordered priorities (Col 3 :1-10) Paul urges believers raised with Christ to seek things above, putting off old self. Repentance reprograms desires—scripture becomes delight, prayer breathing, holiness beauty. Time reallocates: early mornings once spent scrolling now adore Psalm 119; money diverts from vanity to missions. Christ's supremacy dethrones idols of applause or comfort. Though temptations persist, their magnetic pull weakens as superior joy in God strengthens. Monitoring shifting affections becomes diagnostic gauge: if sin's sweetness revives, repentance must deepen. Thus inward realignment is not optional add-on but primary fruit dwarfing external compliance.

6.5.2 Outward restitution: Zacchaeus as case study (Luke 19 :8-9) Zacchaeus's repentance sprouted generosity—half his goods to poor and fourfold restitution. Law required double or fourfold return, so his offer exceeded obligation, revealing transformed heart. Restitution validates sincerity; stolen money returned, lies publicly corrected, damaged reputations rebuilt. Companies embracing gospel may repay unfair profits; churches confess historic complicity in racism. While some harms can't be fully undone, repentant people pursue maximum possible repair, trusting grace for remainder. Such acts silence skeptics who demand tangible proof. Salvation pronouncement followed Zacchaeus's pledge, illustrating link between outward fruit and kingdom entry.

6.5.3 Community impact: reconciled relationships, justice pursued, holiness normalized

Repentance rarely remains private; it ripples outward, mending marriages, healing church splits, transforming neighborhoods. Ephesians 4 depicts repentant thieves laboring to give. In revivals crime rates drop, debts repaid, taverns empty. Holy norms shift peer expectations—porn jokes fade, gossip shunned, prayer meetings flourish. Justice initiatives sprout: trafficking survivors aided, poverty addressed, creation care embraced. These communal fruits verify revival authenticity more than ecstatic experiences. They reflect kingdom invasion, signposting wider renewal when Christ returns. Therefore churches encouraging repentance must also build structures—benevolence funds, reconciliation teams—to steward its social outflow.

6.5.4 Missional overflow: repentant people becoming heralds of the call to repent

The woman at the well, having repented, ran to town inviting neighbors to meet Messiah (John 4 :28-29). Grateful lepers proclaimed healing (Luke 17 :15). Repentant hearts cannot hoard mercy; they echo Baptist's cry, urging others to flee wrath. Evangelism rooted in personal turning exudes authenticity—witnesses speak of tasted grace, not borrowed concepts. Moreover, ongoing repentance fuels humility, preventing judgmental tone. Mission agencies birthed from revival histories testify: when church repents, global outreach surges. Thus repentance not only restores but recruits, turning formerly self-absorbed sinners into ambassadors of reconciliation.

6.6 Repentance and the Means of Grace

6.6.1 Word: how Scripture exposes, promises, and guides the turning heart

David pleaded, "Open my eyes" (Ps 119 :18) because scripture both wounds and heals. Law sections diagnose sin; promises unveil pardon; narratives model restored failures—Peter, Manasseh. Regular reading keeps conscience tender; memorization arms believers against relapse (Ps 119 :11). Preaching functions similarly, a weekly lever prying hearts from idols. Small-group Bible study offers reflective accountability. Without the Word, repentance decays into emotion; with it, turning gains direction and durability, for "Your word is a lamp to my feet" (Ps 119 :105).

6.6.2 Prayer: confession, lament, and petitions for ongoing renewal (Ps 51) Prayer voices repentance, moving from silent regret to relational dialogue. Psalm 51 models confession (naming sin), appeal to mercy, request for clean heart, and vow to teach transgressors. Lament psalms legitimize grief over corporate sins. Daily examen prayers review thoughts and actions, prompting micro-repentance. Prayer also asks for fresh desire, acknowledging inability to change alone. In intercession, believers repent on behalf of communities (Dan 9 :4-19), aligning with priestly calling. Thus prayer fuels and evidences continual turning, weaving repentance into worship rhythm.

6.6.3 Lord's Table and Baptism: sacramental rhythms that rehearse death and rising Baptism dramatizes initial repentance—burial of old self, resurrection in Christ (Rom 6 :3-4). The Lord's Supper invites ongoing self-examination (1 Cor 11 :28): believers recall broken body, confess fresh failures, and receive grace anew. These sacraments guard against disembodied spirituality, sealing repentance in water, bread, wine. They also foster communal accountability— public vows deter secret sin. Abuse occurs when taken lightly, but rightly used they anchor repentance in tangible gospel reminders, strengthening assurance and resolve.

6.6.4 Fellowship and discipline: community safeguards against relapse Isolation breeds relapse. Hebrews 3 :13 prescribes daily encouragement to prevent hardening. Confessional friendships allow rapid confession; mentors ask probing questions. Corporate discipline, though painful, aims to restore by escalating warnings to awaken straying saints. Success stories testify: addicts sustained sobriety when plugged into small groups; marriages healed under elder guidance. Thus community operates like guardrails along repentance road, catching wobbling pilgrims before cliffs beckon.

6.7 Pastoral Guidance for Leading People into Repentance

6.7.1 Law-then-gospel cadence: wounding to heal without manipulation Preachers emulate divine pattern—Sinai precedes Calvary. They expose sin through scripture, illustrations, probing application, yet quickly lift eyes to the cross, lest hearers drown. Tone combines gravity and hope. Avoiding shame tactics, they rely on Spirit to convict. They personalize without singling out embarrassingly; they invite response through prayer stations, counseling rooms, baptisms. Effective sermons climax not in applause but in silence pregnant with decision. Follow-up materials (booklets, mentoring) extend sermon impact, guiding seekers through repentance journey.

6.7.2 Counseling cases—addiction, bitterness, hidden immorality: tailored pathways of turn-and-trust Addicts require medical referrals, accountability software, and gospel identity replacing idol pleasure. Bitter saints need to lament hurts, meditate on God's justice, practice forgiveness rituals. Secret immorality necessitates confession, boundaries, perhaps job changes. Counselors diagnose idol roots—comfort, control, approval—and prescribe specific disciplines. They celebrate incremental victories, reminding counselees that sanctification is marathon. They also address shame, applying Romans 8 :1 balm repeatedly. Customized care transforms general repentance principles into concrete life change.

6.7.3 Corporate moments: solemn assemblies, renewal weekends, and responsive liturgies Churches sometimes need dedicated seasons of corporate repentance—fasting days, confession services, prayer summits. Historical precedents (Ezra 9, Neh 8-9) show Scripture reading fueling tears and covenant renewal. Modern renewal weekends integrate teaching, testimonies, silence, and symbolic acts—nailing sins to cross boards, washing feet. Responsive liturgies weaving lament psalms, Kyrie eleison chants, and assurance readings can normalize repentance. Such events recalibrate culture, signaling that holiness matters more than programming excellence.

6.7.4 Post-repentance care: assurance, accountability, and integrating returnees into service Newly repentant believers often face guilt echoes and temptation waves. Pastors affirm them with promises—Micah 7 :19, 1 John 1 :9—while establishing accountability triads. They encourage service: forgiven women accompany Jesus, demoniac proclaims to Decapolis. Engaging gifts cements identity shift from spectator to servant, leveraging gratitude for kingdom. Churches pair returnees with mentors, schedule check-ins, and celebrate milestones. Thus initial repentance blossoms into discipled perseverance, guarding against relapse and maximizing restored joy.

6.8 Eschatological Urgency and the Open Door

6.8.1 "Today, if you hear His voice": the time-barred offer (Heb 3 :15) The wilderness generation died outside promise because they delayed belief. Author of Hebrews warns contemporary hearers not to harden hearts. Repentance window is finite—life span, Spirit's striving, Christ's return. Procrastination gambles with an unknown expiry date. Gospel preaching therefore carries *today* urgency, not tomorrow suggestion. Altar calls, baptism invitations, and personal evangelism must reflect end-times seriousness, awakening lethargic hearts to seize mercy while door stands open.

6.8.2 Last-days warnings to churches—Ephesus, Laodicea, Thyatira (Rev 2-3) Jesus' letters expose loveless orthodoxy, lukewarm complacency, unchecked immorality, prescribing repentance or lampstand removal. These missives prove that even true churches face judgment if unrepentant. They also reveal gracious discipline: gold refined by fire, meals shared with knocking Savior. Studying these letters equips congregations to self-assess—love temperature, doctrinal purity, moral integrity—and to repent corporately before divine visitation. Eschatological hope motivates holiness, because believers long to hear "Well done."

6.8.3 Finality of hardening: the sober mystery of judicial blindness (Rom 1 :24-28)

Paul describes God giving rebels over to desires—a chilling form of judgment where repentance becomes humanly impossible. Pharaoh's serial hardening illustrates trajectory: initial stubbornness invites divine reinforcement until release vanishes. This mystery instills holy fear: no one controls repentance clock. Thus while alive, every sinner should hasten to respond, lest repeated refusal calcify will. Believers intercede for loved ones, aware that only Spirit can reverse seal. Preachers plead passionately, conscious of stakes.

6.8.4 Global call before cosmic closure: repentance as prelude to the day of the Lord (Acts 17 :30-31)

Paul grounds universal repentance demand in coming judgment by risen Man. Mission impulse flows from this eschatological sequence: warning first, then wrath. Peter explains divine delay as mercy, "not wishing any to perish but all to reach repentance" (2 Pet 3 :9). Every evangelistic endeavor—Bible translation, church planting—extends this merciful pause. Yet gospel witness will eventually reach nations, and day will dawn like thief. Living with that timeline infuses urgency into daily interactions and sustains missionaries amid hardship, knowing their labors expedite kingdom consummation.

Conclusion

Repentance is both diamond and doorway: diamond, because its facets—mind change, heart sorrow, will surrender—sparkle with Spirit-wrought beauty; doorway, because it ushers penitent souls into the wide country of grace where obedience becomes delight. From ancient prophets to apostolic preachers, the summons has never varied, nor has the promise withheld: whoever turns finds pardon, renewal, and unfading joy. Counterfeits abound—regret without change, ritual without surrender, license disguised as grace—yet Scripture's bright criteria and the Spirit's faithful searching keep the path clear. Means of grace sustain the posture;

fellowship upholds the resolve; mission overflows the gratitude. Time, however, is limited: today's open door will not swing forever. Therefore hear, turn, live—and add your voice to the anthem that reverberates from Bethlehem's manger through Calvary's cross to New Jerusalem's throne: "Salvation belongs to our God who sits on the throne, and to the Lamb" (Rev 7 :10).

Chapter 7. Fleeing from the Wrath to Come

No one boards a lifeboat unless convinced the vessel beneath their feet is sinking. Likewise, the gospel's appeal to run for safety resonates only when the soul perceives that the whole present order—its systems, securities, and pleasures—is already ablaze with judgment (2 Pet 3:10–12). After conviction (Chapter 5) reveals sin's guilt and repentance (Chapter 6) bends the knee, a further movement remains: sustained flight from wrath. Fleeing is not frantic despair; it is the sober, hope-laden sprint of a traveler who has glimpsed both the coming storm and the open refuge. Scripture presents this flight as wisdom's signature posture. Lot left Sodom at dawn; Israel departed Egypt under blood-stained doorposts; first-century disciples evacuated Jerusalem when Roman eagles shadowed its walls. Each narrative embeds a universal principle: God's warnings are invitations to life, and history is littered with the graves of those who lingered. In our age of technological optimism and moral fog, we need once more to recover the urgency that spurred early believers to live like refugees—light-footed, watchful, and generous—while urging neighbors onto the last train of mercy. The following pages chart the biblical pattern, the obstacles, the route, and the communal dynamics of that ongoing exodus.

Prelude - The Last Train Pulling Out of the Station

The image of flight in Scripture—from Lot's sprint out of Sodom to Hebrews' "strong encouragement" Genesis 19 paints a harrowing dawn: angels grabbing Lot's wrists, hustling him beyond city limits while sulfur clouds gathered overhead. "Escape for your life; do not look back" (Gen 19:17). That imperative echoes through redemptive history. When Pharaoh's chariots closed in, Israel fled through walls of water (Ex 14:21–27). Centuries later, author of Hebrews exhorts believers to "flee for refuge to lay hold upon the hope set before us," a hope compared to an anchor lodged within the veil (Heb 6:18–19). Flight, therefore, is not cowardice but covenant obedience—a decisive relocation from doomed terrain to promised security. Each episode underscores God's two-fold mercy: He warns before He strikes, and He provides a means of escape sturdy enough for any who will trust. The decisive question in every generation is not whether warning exists, but whether listeners will turn warning into movement.

Why wrath is both future and even now "revealed" (Rom 1:18) Paul insists that God's wrath "is revealed" in the present tense against ungodliness—seen in disordered passions, fractured societies, and darkened minds (Rom 1:24–32). These creeping judgments foreshadow a climactic outpouring on the last day (Rom 2:5–8). Thus wrath operates like a horizon-spanning storm: distant thunder reminds hearers to seek shelter before lightning strikes overhead. Contemporary anxieties—pandemics, environmental crises, geopolitical tremors—are not random; they are birth-pangs (Mark 13:8), gentle escalations designed to yank fingers from earplugs. To interpret present disorder merely as political mishap or natural cycle is to sleep through a siren. Wise hearts read history theologically, recognizing God's reveal of displeasure as prelude to final unveiling (apokalypsis) when every hidden deed meets righteous fire (Rev 20:11–15).

Panic versus prudent haste: distinguishing godly urgency from fleshly frenzy Biblical flight is marked by haste—Israel ate unleavened bread, sandals strapped, staffs ready (Ex 12:11). Yet haste may decay into panic if not yoked to faith. Panic hoards toilet paper, spews conspiracy theories, and tramples the weak. Prudent haste obeys commands promptly, entrusting outcomes to providence. Jesus' counsel to disciples—"when you see Jerusalem surrounded... flee to the mountains" (Luke 21:20–21)—was calm, detailed, and practical, resulting in believers' escape to Pella before Rome's siege. Similarly, Christians today oppose wrath not with bunkers and canned beans but with rapid obedience: turning off porn, reconciling grudges, sharing Christ before death steals the opportunity. Godly urgency keeps priorities eternal while hands stay gentle; it runs without shoving.

7.1 The Bible's Pattern of Urgent Escape

7.1.1 Noah's ark: divine blueprint for timely obedience (Gen 6–7) At a time when rain was science fiction, God ordered ark construction on dry ground. For 120 years Noah hammered boards, condemned the world by faith, and beckoned neighbors to safety (Heb 11:7). His obedience illustrates three elements of flight: (1) revelation precedes strategy—God, not human ingenuity, defined the escape plan; (2) preparation happens under scoffing—mockers always misread mercy's delay as evidence of myth (2 Pet 3:3–5); (3) deadline arrives abruptly—on the day Noah entered, "the LORD shut him in," and fountains burst (Gen 7:13–16). Modern parallels abound: Christ, greater Noah, offers Himself as living ark; His church nails planks through preaching; baptism signals entry. To postpone boarding because skies remain blue is folly squared, for the same clouds that rained judgment lifted the ark to safety.

7.1.2 Passover night: sandals on feet, staff in hand (Ex 12:11) Israel's exodus rehearsal mandated readiness—belt fastened, loins girded. Salvation would occur at midnight; dilly-dallying risked first-born bloodshed. Paul reinterprets Passover for Corinthian believers, urging them to purge old

leaven while celebrating the Lamb already slain (1 Cor 5:7–8). Believers thus live in permanent departure mode—identity tied to journey, not Egypt's menu. Sanctification flows from this migrant mindset: why cherish sin souvenirs from a country scheduled for plagues? Every communion table whispers, "Eat quickly; we're traveling soon." Eschatological flight fuels ethical vigilance.

7.1.3 Rahab's scarlet cord: personal refuge amid corporate judgment (Josh 2) Jericho's walls would fall, yet a prostitute's window dangled red rope—a prophecy in yarn. Rahab fled wrath not by emigration but by covenant sign: remain inside marked house. Her story shows that escape is sometimes stationary: union with covenant symbol secures safety while destruction swirls outside. The cord foreshadows Christ's blood displayed publicly (Rom 3:25). Family members gathered under her roof just as believers invite relatives into gospel sphere. Judgment day will likewise honor such visible allegiance, passing over those sheltered beneath crimson righteousness.

7.1.4 Jesus' Olivet warning: flight from doomed Jerusalem as prototype (Matt 24:15–22) When the Roman eagle (abomination of desolation) perched on temple parapets, disciples remembered their Master's instructions and fled south-east. Eusebius records wholesale Christian evacuation, sparing thousands from 70 AD slaughter. This event illustrates prophetic words functioning as literal evacuation orders and eschatological templates. The fall of Jerusalem prefigures global consummation: a local cataclysm validating Jesus' lordship and modeling believer response—discern signs, accept loss of property, prioritize life over relics. Today, believers must similarly loosen grip on temporal securities once Spirit indicates departure, whether from toxic relationships, corrupt industries, or idolatrous nationalism.

7.2 The Certainty and Nearness of Impending Wrath

7.2.1 Eschatological vocabulary—day of the Lord, hour of trial, great tribulation Prophets compress a range of judgments into the phrase "day of the LORD" (Joel 2:31), signaling both historical interventions (Babylon's invasion) and final reckoning. Jesus and John diversify imagery—"hour of trial" (Rev 3:10) for localized tests, "great tribulation" (Matt 24:21) for unparalleled upheaval. While interpreters debate chronology, all concur on inevitability: a scheduled period when divine patience expires and accounts settle. Terms like "hour" underscore brevity; wrath, though fierce, is not capricious torture but swift judicial verdict. For saints, awareness of God's timetable fosters sobriety without dread; for rebels, it removes plea of ignorance.

7.2.2 Apocalyptic birth-pangs: wars, plagues, and cultural unraveling (Mark 13:8) Jesus likens end-time convulsions to labor—painful yet purposeful, increasing in intensity until new creation crowns. Wars remind that peace treaties cannot heal human depravity; pandemics expose mortality beneath medical triumphalism; moral revolutions display Romans 1 spiral. These signs are not random; they are contractions causing the church to groan and Spirit to intercede (Rom 8:22–23). Misinterpreting them breeds either alarmism (date-setting prophets) or apathy (scoffing intellectuals). Properly received, they catalyze evangelism: contractions quicken pace of midwives; similarly, signs quicken witness before the water breaks into judgment.

7.2.3 Personal eschatology: death as the individual day of reckoning (Heb 9:27) Even if global finale tarries, every human faces private apocalypse at death, after which judgment follows. Youthful vigor, medical insurance, and exercise cannot guarantee tomorrow. Jesus' parable of rich fool—Barns bigger, breath shorter—illustrates sudden personal doomsday (Luke 12:16–21). Therefore urgency is universal; elderly and adolescent alike stand minutes from tribunal. Flight from wrath is thus not merely end-times escapism but daily necessity. Mortality statistics preach louder than apocalyptic charts; one hundred percent die, and only those hidden in Christ live again unto glory.

7.2.4 Cosmic finale: final judgment before the white throne (Rev 20:11–15) John envisions earth and sky fleeing before Judge whose face none can resist. Books open, revealing exhaustive records; a separate book—the Lamb's—overrides guilt for those enrolled. This scene unites moral realism (deeds matter) with evangelical hope (grace triumphs). Hell's lake of fire is ultimate wrath habitat for unrepentant. To preach heaven without this counterpart is malpractice. Certainty of throne means every apology unsaid, every injustice unpunished, will surface. Believers rejoice that Christ stands as Advocate (1 John 2:1), yet they also tremble for neighbors. Knowledge of cosmic finale fuels missionary passion, humanitarian justice, and personal holiness.

7.3 Voices Crying "Flee!": Heralds of Divine Warning

7.3.1 John the Baptist's ax-at-the-root sermon (Matt 3:7–12) Leather-clad prophet confronted religious elites, calling them vipers and depicting Messiah's winnowing fork separating wheat from chaff. His call to "bear fruit" challenged hereditary confidence: Abrahamic lineage cannot deflect falling ax. Modern heralds must likewise expose nominal Christianity—baptism certificates cannot absorb wrath. John's ministry models balance: urgency drenched in hope, for baptism signaled washing soon ratified by Jesus' sin-bearing cross. Effective preaching today retains that edge—clear, concrete, courageously personal—so that hearers feel ground rumble beneath fig-leaf piety.

7.3.2 Apostolic appeals—Peter at Pentecost, Paul in Athens (Acts 2; 17) Peter, fresh from Spirit fire, accused crowd of murdering Messiah, yet immediately offered forgiveness and Spirit gift. Three thousand fled wrath into baptismal waters. Later, Paul engaged philosophers, announcing appointed day of judgment and resurrection proof. Some sneered, others pondered, a few joined. Apostolic pattern combines contextual bridge-building with uncompromising ultimatum. Street preachers and academic apologists alike must fuse cultural fluency with divine ultimatum: flight is rational because resurrection is historical, judgment scheduled, and refuge available.

7.3.3 Reformers and revivalists—Luther's thunder, Whitefield's tears
Martin Luther thundered against indulgence industry, insisting "true repentance has nothing to do with outward penance but inner change." His printed tracts became fire alarms across Europe. Whitefield wept as he warned coal miners, face blackened by dust turned white by tears. Emotion varied—thunder, tears—but message matched: flee wrath through Christ alone. Studying these movements reveals that God renews warning ministry each era, adapting accents but preserving core. Our generation requires digital heralds leveraging podcasts, but authenticity— deep holiness, sacrificial love—remains microphone for Spirit unction.

7.3.4 Contemporary prophets: the church's vocation to sound the alarm
Prophetic gifting did not expire; pastors, artists, activists now relay warnings via pulpit, canvas, and documentary. Church must steward this vocation, avoiding shrill sensationalism yet refusing domestication. Silence on hell or cultural idols betrays mandate. When believers advocate for unborn, trafficked, or racially oppressed, they echo divine alarm against systemic sin. Evangelistic urgency, ethical protest, and intercessory lament harmonize into trumpet blast summoning society to repentance. Congregations that relegate prophecy to relics risk becoming museums rather than watchtowers.

7.4 Common Obstacles Hindering Flight

7.4.1 Affection for Sodom: lingering love of worldly pleasures
Lot's wife illustrates tragedy of half-hearted exodus—body leaving, heart staying. Jesus commemorated

her with terse warning, "Remember Lot's wife" (Luke 17:32). Modern Sodoms—porn streams, consumer culture, status loops—seduce fleeing hearts to glance back. Solution lies not in stoic willpower but superior delight: Moses counted reproach of Christ greater wealth than Egypt's treasures (Heb 11:26). Regular worship, sabbath rhythms, and generous giving untangle affection by directing joy toward eternal pleasures. No one turns back if captivated by better homeland (Heb 11:16).

7.4.2 Skeptical scoffers—"Where is the promise of His coming?" (2 Pet 3:4) Intellectual pride mocks apocalypse as Bronze-Age myth, citing centuries of delay. Peter counters: delay equals mercy; past flood proves precedent; promised conflagration awaits appointed hour. Christian engagement with skeptics must combine apologetics—historical resurrection evidence—with moral challenge: what if conscience's nagging sense of right and wrong predicts tribunal? Ultimately, the Spirit must unmask willful ignorance. Believers guard against internal scoffing by cultivating eschatological imagination through book of Revelation readings and hymns like "Lo, He Comes with Clouds Descending."

7.4.3 Paralysis of procrastination and the myth of tomorrow (Prov 27:1) Felix trembled but postponed (Acts 24:25). Every unconverted reader likely intends to repent—later. Procrastination stems from unbelief that wrath is near or that grace could satisfy. Puritan Joseph Alleine wrote, "Thy soul is for ever lost if thou be not changed without delay." Overcoming delay requires vivid preaching of death's certainty, testimonies of sudden endings, and personal accountability. Discipleship relationships push friends to calendar spiritual steps—baptism date, confession meeting—turning vague intention into concrete action.

7.4.4 Counterfeit shelters—religiosity, morality, and ideological causes Israel trusted temple architecture; Pharisees trusted law minutiae; moderns trust activism or mindfulness. These shelters crumble on judgment day because righteousness standards exceed performance.

Jesus likens such refuge to house on sand (Matt 7:26–27). Pastors must expose insufficiency of moral causes detached from gospel—feeding poor without fleeing wrath still leaves souls lost. True shelter involves union with Christ; all else is fig-leaf bunker. Evaluating foundation requires honest audits: upon what does my peace rest—metrics or Messiah?

7.5 The Route of Escape: Union with Christ

7.5.1 The city of refuge motif fulfilled in the crucified-risen Lord Mosaic law established six towns where accidental killers could flee (Num 35). Entrance required crossing threshold before avenger caught them. Hebrews applies this type to Jesus—the better refuge guaranteeing access beyond veil (Heb 6:18–20). Unlike cities restricted by geography, Christ is omnipresent refuge; unlike manslaughter cases, He shelters willful rebels by bearing penalty Himself. Evangelists therefore point not to church membership or self-reform but to living Person whose wounds constitute impregnable walls.

7.5.2 Entering the gate by repentance and faith (John 10:9) Jesus calls Himself the door; whoever enters finds salvation and pasture. Entry mechanics are simple yet profound: repent (turn) and believe (trust). Intellectual assent alone is insufficient; demons believe facts (Jas 2:19). Neither is mere sorrow enough (Judas). Saving faith, inseparable from repentance, banks entire destiny on Christ's atonement, welcomes lordship, and receives Spirit. Baptism publicly dramatizes this passage, water functioning not as soap but as Red-Sea threshold—slavery drowned, new life surfaced.

7.5.3 Baptism as Red-Sea crossing—formal transfer of realm (Rom 6:3–4) Paul ties baptism to burial and resurrection, declaring old self crucified. Early Christians regarded font as watery grave where Pharaoh's tyranny drowned. This sacrament doesn't exempt from future obedience, but it stamps passport: realm of darkness to kingdom of Son (Col 1:13). Newly baptized disciples must learn to live out identity—no longer slaves to sin, therefore fight temptation from victory ground. Pastoral instruction ensures symbol's substance: teaching union with Christ, not mere rite performance, preserves refuge reality.

7.5.4 The Lord's Table as ongoing rehearsal of covered wrath (1 Cor 11:26) Communion proclaims Lord's death "until He comes," bridging past rescue and future judgment. Cup symbolizes wrath absorbed (Luke 22:42). Each sip rehearses shelter—danger outside, peace inside. Self-examination prevents presumption; unworthy partaking invites discipline mirroring miniature wrath (1 Cor 11:30–32) so larger wrath need not fall. Thus Table both comforts and cautions, sustaining flight by reminding pilgrims of purchased security and urging holy travel.

7.6 Pilgrim Ethics: Living Between Flight and Arrival

7.6.1 Exiles and sojourners: adopting a travel-light mentality (1 Pet 2:11) Peter labels believers "sojourners and exiles," stabilizing identity in heaven's registry. Travelers pack minimally; Christians view possessions as tools, not trophies. Hebrews commends saints who joyfully accepted plunder of property knowing they had better inheritance (Heb 10:34). Practical outworkings include simplicity, generosity, career choices shaped by mission more than advancement. Travel-light ethos accelerates obedience—no anchors delaying Spirit's call.

7.6.2 Watchfulness and prayer: lamps trimmed, hearts awake (Luke 12:35–40) Jesus' parable of master's return highlights vigilance: servants keep lamps burning, belts girded. Watchfulness combines alert discernment of times with active prayer, lest hearts grow dull through dissipation (Luke 21:34–36). Daily examen, weekly sabbath, and corporate prayer nights maintain flame. Neglect yields spiritual drowsiness, making alarm bells sound distant. Early church greeting "Maranatha!" embodied constant readiness; reviving that watchword fortifies twenty-first-century disciples.

7.6.3 Holiness hastening the day (2 Pet 3:11–12) Peter links holy conduct to speeding parousia—a mysterious synergy wherein obedience cooperates with God's timeline. Missions, intercession, and justice work apparently fill quota God sovereignly set, after which trumpet sounds. Therefore ethical living is not mere waiting pastime but pivotal component accelerating new-creation dawn. Purity, generosity, evangelism, and peacemaking become eschatological catalysts, proving that fleeing wrath is not passive hide-and-wait but active kingdom advance.

7.6.4 Mercy ministry as fire-alarm for neighbors in danger (Jude 23) Jude urges believers to "save others, snatching them out of fire," blending compassion and courage. Practical mercy—feeding hungry, welcoming refugees—creates relational bridges enabling gospel plea. Service also visualizes God's kindness, making wrath warnings credible. Early church rescued unwanted infants left to die, contrasting empire's cruelty; modern equivalents include crisis-pregnancy centers, anti-trafficking work, and racial reconciliation initiatives. Each act says, "Judgment is near, but mercy is nearer—come with us."

7.7 The Church as an Ark of Refuge

7.7.1 Gospel preaching as plank-by-plank construction Noah's hammer echoes in pulpits where Christ is heralded. Every sermon faithful to text nails another board to ark hull. Evangelistic Bible studies, podcasts, children's catechisms—all extensions of building project. Church budgets allocate funds for missions because unfinished planks threaten leaks. Thus, preaching is not entertainment but maritime engineering safeguarding souls from deluge.

7.7.2 Discipline and doctrine—keeping the vessel seaworthy Rotten boards—heresy, unchecked sin—compromise ark integrity. Jesus commands churches to address offenders lest lampstand removed. Creeds and confessions caulk seams, preventing cultural currents from eroding gospel. Elders function as maintenance crew, examining theology and practice. Seaworthy vessel survives storms; compromised churches sink, taking passengers with them. Therefore love demands rigorous upkeep.

7.7.3 Hospitality: swinging the door wide for every repentant fugitive Ark door remained open until last moment; likewise, churches welcome weary sinners without prequalification except repentance and faith. Hospitality dinners, accessible liturgies, multilingual services widen entry. After conversion, integration teams foster belonging, combating temptation to slip back into world. Diversity within ark—Jew, Gentile, elite, poor—displays universality of refuge. Closed cliques contradict door theology; generous inclusion advertises gospel.

7.7.4 Sacrificial unity: the witness of a rescued community (John 17:23) Jesus prayed unity would convince world of divine mission. Ark passengers live in tight quarters; conflict inevitable, but shared deliverance creates superlative bond. Forgiving seventy-times-seven, bearing burdens, and honoring differences illustrate kingdom now. Watching world wonders: "What power reconciles enemies?" Answer: blood stronger than tribalism. Such unity magnetizes outsiders toward safe harbor before flood arrives.

Conclusion

The call to flee from wrath is not archaic rhetoric but the most rational directive given the moral physics of the universe. Every page of Scripture pulses with urgency: prophets shouting from walls, apostles pleading in marketplaces, and Jesus Himself weeping over cities unaware of approaching fires. Flight demands both swiftness and precision, for only one route—union with the crucified-risen Son—guarantees escape. Along that route pilgrims must shed Sodom's trinkets, resist scoffers' lullabies, and travel light under the weight of glory. They walk together, plank-builders and door-keepers in a communal ark whose holiness, unity, and hospitality advertise God's open door. Each contraction of history, each tombstone in the cemetery, each headline of upheaval crescendos the same refrain: "Escape for your life, do not look back." Those who heed will find, to their astonishment, that the refuge is not merely a shelter but a banquet hall—and the One who built it is also the One who bore the storm. May every reader join the company of haste-filled, peace-secured fugitives, and may their footprints guide multitudes onto the last train of redeeming grace before whistle fades and doors close forever.

Chapter 8. Christ the Sure Refuge

Every storm-battered generation eventually asks where an unshakable shelter can be found. The gospel's answer is not a philosophy, a political program, or even a code of conduct, but a Person whose nail-scarred hands have already absorbed the full fury of the tempest. Christ is the sure refuge because every biblical image of protection—ark, rock, city of refuge, Passover blood, mother bird's wings—ultimately converges on Him. The following pages explore that convergence in detail. We will examine what makes Jesus singularly qualified to shield sinners, how His cross and resurrection constructed impregnable walls, why union with Him guarantees present peace and future glory, and how believers enter and abide within those walls. Each subsection lingers over one aspect of the Savior's saving work, not as an abstract doctrine but as the living architecture of safety for people who have already heard the thunder of coming wrath. May this chapter widen our wonder, steady our faith, and equip our lips to beckon others into the shelter before the final storm breaks.

Prelude - Shelter in the Storm

From ark to advocate—how every biblical refuge converges on the Son Noah's wooden vessel, hewn from gopher trees, was the first large-scale portrait of salvation by enclosure. Later, Moses would hide in a cleft of rock while Yahweh's glory passed by, safe only because a hand covered the opening (Ex 33:22). The tabernacle's mercy-seat crowned a box that itself echoed the ark theme: stay under the blood-sprinkled lid and live. Each refuge, whether floating on floodwaters or anchored on Sinai, anticipates the day when the eternal Word took flesh to become both ark and mercy-seat in one incarnate Person (John 1:14; Rom 3:25). The typological stream narrows to a single fountainhead when Christ, our true Advocate, pleads His own blood before the Father (1 John 2:1–2). Thus the story line of Scripture does not present multiple optional shelters; it funnels humanity toward one decisive sanctuary. To read the Bible without seeing that convergence is to miss its central architecture and to forfeit the only reliable hiding place when judgment waters rise.

"Rock of Ages": imagery of cleft-in-the-rock safety (Ex 33:22; 1 Cor 10:4) God hid Moses in a rent rock, foreshadowing a greater fissure opened at Calvary when the last Adam was struck for His people. Paul draws the line explicitly: "That Rock was Christ" (1 Cor 10:4). A cleft is paradoxical—a wound in granite that becomes a womb of security. Hymn writer Augustus Toplady caught the logic: "Let me hide myself in Thee." The smitten side of Jesus offers space wide enough for the chief of sinners yet narrow enough that self-righteous baggage cannot squeeze through. Like Moses, believers glimpse divine glory only from within this fracture; outside it, holiness would incinerate them. Consequently, every gospel invitation is an echo of God's directive to Moses: "Stand on the rock." Those who heed find that judgment's fire cannot reach through the wounded granite of Immanuel's flesh, making the cross the safest place in the universe precisely because it was once the most dangerous.

The exclusivity of the shelter and the wideness of its welcome Jesus stated without apology, "No one comes to the Father except through Me" (John 14:6). That exclusivity is not narrow-mindedness but the simple fact that only one door has been cut in the storm-wall. Yet the doorway's width is measured by divine mercy, not human prejudice: "Whoever comes to Me I will never cast out" (John 6:37). The same crossbar that shuts out self-salvation swings wide for repentant thieves, foreign eunuchs, and once-murderous persecutors. The gospel therefore contradicts both pluralism—which offers many inadequate shelters—and tribalism, which tries to reserve the real shelter for a few. In Christ, exclusivity and inclusivity reconcile: there is only one refuge, but its gates remain open until the last moment, and the ticket is free for all who acknowledge their bankruptcy. The urgent mission of the church is to keep that welcome clear, neither retreating into sectarian enclaves nor diluting the message into impotent relativism.

8.1 The Person of the Savior: Fully God, Fully Man

8.1.1 Deity strong enough to absorb infinite wrath (John 1:1; Col 2:9) Wrath against cosmic treason demands a payment proportionate to divine honor. Only someone sharing that infinite dignity could satisfy the debt without being crushed forever. John opens his Gospel by asserting the Word's full deity—He "was God" and therefore unlimited in worth (John 1:1). Paul echoes, "In Him the whole fullness of deity dwells bodily" (Col 2:9). Christ's divine nature supplies the vast reservoir of value needed to quench an ocean of righteous anger. Finite creatures drowning in their own sins require an infinite lifeguard, not merely a sympathetic peer. Deity also guarantees immutability, so the refuge cannot erode; omnipotence, so no foe can breach its walls; omnipresence, so the shelter is accessible from any longitude or century. Every attribute of Godhead undergirds the security of redemption, assuring saints that no unforeseen evil can outmuscle their Protector.

8.1.2 Humanity near enough to substitute for Adam's race (Heb 2:14–17) Deity alone could pay, but humanity had to pay because humanity had sinned. The eternal Son therefore added a full human nature, entering Mary's womb without surrendering divine glory. Hebrews highlights the necessity: "Since the children share in flesh and blood, He Himself likewise partook" so He could die in their place (Heb 2:14). Substitution depends on likeness; goats and calves were temporary placeholders pointing to the day when the forfeited human life would be repaid by a flawless human life. Jesus wept, sweated, hungered, and bled—crucial credentials for standing in the dock on our behalf. His obedience under our limitations forges the righteousness imputed to believers (Rom 5:19). The God-Man thus forms a living bridge, His nailed feet planted on earth, His everlasting arms stretching into heaven—uniting realms so rebels may walk across.

8.1.3 The hypostatic union as foundation of all saving efficacy The council of Chalcedon confessed Christ "in two natures, without confusion, change, division, or separation." That mystery—one Person subsisting in both natures—prevents split-level salvation. Were the natures divided, human sufferings might not access divine merit; were they confused, deity might dilute into sufferable fragility. The union secures that every act—each tear, word, and drop of blood—belongs to the one Lord of glory (Acts 20:28). Consequently, the refuge is not modular (part human comfort, part divine pardon) but integrated. Prayer ascends through a Mediator who feels our weakness and wields omnipotence simultaneously. Worship erupts because the Carpenter enthroned is still the Logos eternal. All heresies that diminish either nature chip holes in the walls of safety; orthodox Christology keeps the shelter airtight.

8.1.4 Emmanuel's sympathy: a refuge that understands our frame (Heb 4:15) Safety can feel like isolation if the walls are cold and impersonal, but Christ's refuge pulses with sympathy. Having been tempted in every way yet without sin, He is touched by the feeling of our infirmities (Heb 4:15). He knows the pull of despair, the sting of betrayal, the ache of hunger, and the wrench of death. Therefore, fleeing sinners do not arrive at a clinical bunker but at a warmly lit hospice where the Physician bears identical scars. His empathy does not weaken security; it reinforces it by assuring us that no bruise or memory disqualifies entrance. The One who guards the gate also washes the feet of those who enter. In every dark corridor of the shelter there echoes this promise: "I will never leave you nor forsake you" (Heb 13:5).

8.2 The Cross: Shelter Constructed With Crimson Timber

8.2.1 Penal substitution—justice satisfied, sinners justified (Rom 3:24–26) At Calvary, God displayed Christ as a propitiation "to demonstrate His righteousness... that He might be just and the justifier" (Rom 3:25–26). Justice demanded death; love desired pardon. Penal substitution solves the dilemma by transferring penalty to a willing Substitute. The hammering of Roman spikes was heaven's carpentry, fastening beams into the framework of everlasting safety. Our sins became Christ's legal property; His righteousness becomes ours by faith (2 Cor 5:21). Therefore, condemnation cannot enter the refuge without first condemning the Substitute already executed, which is impossible. Justification is thus more than divine leniency; it is a juridical verdict rooted in executed justice, making the shelter courtroom-proof.

8.2.2 Propitiation versus expiation: wrath averted, guilt removed (1 John 4:10) Propitiation turns away God's wrath; expiation cleanses the sinner's defilement. The cross accomplishes both. John writes, "He loved us and sent His Son to be the propitiation for our sins" (1 John 4:10). Blood on the mercy-seat satisfies holiness, while blood on the sinner washes conscience (Heb 9:14). Refuge, therefore, is not merely a hurricane bunker keeping condemnation outside; it is also an inner bath scrubbing shame from within. Travelers enter not as filthy beggars hiding in a corner but as family dressed in robes washed white (Rev 7:14). Both aspects are vital: without propitiation the storm would still breach; without expiation guilt would rot souls from inside. Christ provides comprehensive coverage—external, internal, eternal.

8.2.3 Covenant curse concentrated on the sin-bearer (Gal 3:13) Moses listed covenant maledictions—exile, famine, hanging on a tree—for lawbreakers (Deut 28). Paul declares that Christ "became a curse for us" by hanging on the tree, absorbing cumulative covenant penalties (Gal 3:13). Like a lightning rod on a fortress turret, the crucified body attracted every bolt of judgment, grounding it forever. This concentration of curse means none is left to strike those inside the walls. The shelter's warranty is written in the crimson ink of cursed blood: "Paid in full." Believers rehearsing this truth silence Satanic accusations and internal legalism, remembering the curse cannot boomerang once God's thunderbolt has found its terminal mark.

8.2.4 The tearing veil: open access into the holy safe-room (Matt 27:51) When Jesus dismissed His spirit, the temple veil ripped from top to bottom—divine hand shattering segregation. Behind the curtain lay the ark's covering mercy-seat, the earthly hotspot of glory. By rending the fabric, God announced that His presence no longer threatened death for those covered by blood. Refuge is thus not merely escape **from** wrath but entrance **to** fellowship. Sinners turned saints move past the bronze altar of atonement into inner courts of communion, welcomed by Fatherly smile. Every prayer whispered in Jesus' name travels this torn-veil corridor straight to the throne (Heb 10:19–22). The shelter, therefore, is not dim exile; it is radiant audience hall.

8.3 Resurrection and Ascension: The Indestructible Foundation

8.3.1 Empty tomb as divine receipt—payment accepted (Rom 4:25) Paul links resurrection to justification: Christ "was raised for our justification" (Rom 4:25). If death was wages for sin, rising on the third day signals zero balance due. The empty tomb is heaven's stamped receipt, displayed where angels once sat on folded grave-clothes. Refuge would wobble if the cross were final but unverified; resurrection cements confidence, proving the shelter earthquake-proof even when stone seals rupture. Whenever doubt rattles windows, believers point to the vacated sepulchre: the payment cleared, the shelter stands.

8.3.2 Ascended High Priest securing continual coverage (Heb 7:24–25) Levitical priests were mortal and multiple; Jesus, by contrast, "holds His priesthood permanently" and "always lives to make intercession" (Heb 7:24-25). Refuge sustainability depends on ongoing priestly maintenance—constant application of atoning blood in heavenly tabernacle. Christ's ascension installs such maintenance eternally. Every second, He pleads accomplished work, ensuring no lapse in protection. Storms intensify? The High Priest's incense thickens. Thus, security is not static wall but dynamic advocacy.

8.3.3 Session at God's right hand: kingly refuge defending citizens (Ps 110:1) "The LORD said to my Lord, 'Sit at my right hand until I make your enemies your footstool'" (Ps 110:1). King Jesus enthroned wields all authority to shield His people. No accusation, demonic assault, or geopolitical persecution can breach His jurisdiction. Refuge walls are buttressed by sovereign decree. Even martyrdom cannot negate security; it escorts saints through valley into closer chambers. The enthroned Lamb shepherds them to springs of living water (Rev 7:17), proving kingship and refuge are two faces of the same ascended majesty.

8.3.4 Firstfruits guarantee of a refuge that swallows death itself (1 Cor 15:20–23) Christ's resurrection inaugurates harvest; He is firstfruits, promising entire crop. The final enemy, death, will be swallowed in victory (1 Cor 15:54–57). A shelter that outlasts everything except death would eventually fail; Christ's outlasts death too. The refuge contains a built-in resurrection chamber where buried saints will rise in glorified bodies. Therefore, Christian funerals, though soaked in grief, resonate with confident hymns. The casket becomes seedpod; the cemetery, garden awaiting spring. Resurrection

turns the refuge from bomb shelter into new-creation embassy.

8.4 Union With Christ: Entering the Safe Stronghold

8.4.1 Spirit-wrought graft into the last Adam (1 Cor 1:30) Salvation is not mere imitation of Jesus but participation in Him. By Spirit baptism believers are grafted into Christ like branches into vine (1 Cor 12:13). Paul exults that God made Christ "our wisdom, righteousness, sanctification, and redemption" (1 Cor 1:30); these blessings flow through union canal. Inside the refuge, identity reshapes: personal résumé replaced by Christ's achievements. Guilt cannot locate the believer because legal coordinates now read "in Christ," a realm outside wrath's jurisdiction. This mystical inclusion surpasses cold forensic transfer; it is living solidarity, heartbeat sharing, destiny intertwining.

8.4.2 Baptismal sign of burial in, and rising with, the Refuge (Rom 6:3–5) Water burial dramatizes union: down with old Adam, up in new Adam. The sacrament is not magical but monumental, a covenant billboard declaring transfer of citizenship. Its retrospective meaning (sins washed) and prospective charge (walk in newness) reinforce refuge identity. Doubting saints recall their baptism like refugees clutching immigration papers. When condemnation whispers, they answer, "I have been baptized into Christ; any charge must pass through Him first."

8.4.3 Mystical marriage—His riches become the bride's dowry (Eph 5:31–32) Paul dares compare human marriage to Christ's union with church. In ancient weddings, the groom's name conferred status and debt relief on the bride. So with Jesus: His obedience credited, His Spirit shared, His home inherited. Covenant oneness also implies mutual belonging; the Refuge claims us even as we claim Him. Devotion and fidelity thus spring not from fear of eviction but from spousal affection. Sanctification is marital delight, not probationary tenancy.

8.4.4 Indwelling Spirit as inner fortification and warranty (Eph 1:13–14) God seals believers with Holy Spirit, "the guarantee of our inheritance." The Greek arrabōn denotes down payment, ensuring full possession later. The Spirit internalizes refuge walls, making heart His temple. Security therefore is double-layered: external Christ for us, internal Spirit in us. Assurance flourishes because the guarantor Himself whispers, "Abba, Father" (Rom 8:15), aligning subjective experience with objective promise. Losing salvation would require the Spirit to default on His own earnest money— impossible.

8.5 The Covenant Guarantees: Promises That Cannot Fail

8.5.1 Better covenant, better mediator, better blood (Heb 8:6) Old covenant relied on human fidelity; new covenant rests on Christ's. Hebrews stacks superlatives: better promises, better sacrifice. Animal blood could annualize safety but never finalize it; Jesus' blood once for all secures everlasting righteousness (Heb 10:14). Covenant superiority is refuge stability; no fine print allows cancellation. Believers read their contract and find Jesus' signature on every clause, written in crimson unerasable ink.

8.5.2 The Father's oath and the Son's surety (Heb 6:17– 20) God, "desiring to show…the unchangeable character of His purpose," swore by Himself, providing double confirmation—promise and oath. Hope thus anchors soul within the veil where Jesus has entered as forerunner. Christ is also surety (Heb 7:22), personally guaranteeing covenant terms on behalf of His people. Unlike human guarantors, He cannot default. If a saint were lost, God would violate His own oath, an absurdity that underscores refuge reliability.

8.5.3 Irrevocable adoption sealing family safety (Rom 8:15–17)
Salvation's legal standing is not mere pardon of criminals but adoption of children. Roman adoption bestowed irrevocable inheritance; disowning an adopted child was illegal. Paul draws on that cultural backdrop: heirs of God, co-heirs with Christ. Discipline may occur, but disinheritance never. The refuge, therefore, feels like home with a Father, not like a safe house with a parole officer. Cardiovascular assurance beats in prayer that begins "Abba"—proof of belonging.

8.5.4 Intercession and advocacy silencing every accusation (1 John 2:1)
When believers sin, Satan prosecutes; Christ, the righteous, advocates. His defense is not relativistic spin but completed atonement—hands lifted exposing indelible wounds. Heavenly courtroom thereby functions perpetually in favor of saints. Earthly consciences mirror verdict, regaining peace as Spirit applies gospel. The refuge includes this legal office open 24 / 7; no allegation lodges for long because Advocate and Judge share the bench.

8.6 Present Blessings Inside the Refuge

8.6.1 No condemnation: conscience cleansed, courtroom closed (Rom 8:1)
To step into Christ is to exit condemnation realm permanently. Though Satan recycles memories, verdict remains "no condemnation." Conscience, cleansed by blood, transitions from prosecution witness to peace umpire (Heb 9:14). Spiritual growth thus proceeds not by fear of re-condemnation but by gratitude-fueled obedience. Saints confess sins not to regain lost status but to restore fellowship, akin to family apology after supper, not courtroom plea-bargain. This freedom fertilizes robust joy and bold access.

8.6.2 Freedom from sin's dominion—new power for holiness (Rom 6:14)
Grace not only forgives but dethrones sin. Inside refuge, tyrant masters lose jurisdiction; believers still battle but under new regime. Habits once unbreakable become vulnerable as Spirit supplies power to put to death

deeds of body (Rom 8:13). Holiness turns from ladder to dance—response to music of redemption. Sanctification, therefore, is in-house renovation, not probationary rent. Every victory over lust or bitterness testifies that the shelter is alive with transforming energy.

8.6.3 Peace that surpasses understanding amidst ongoing storms (Phil 4:7) The refuge does not remove external weather; hurricanes rage until new creation. Yet peace inside exceeds comprehension—guarding hearts like garrison (Phil 4:7). Such shalom flows from settled verdict, sympathetic High Priest, and sovereign King. Paul, chained to guards, sings because chains cannot penetrate refuge walls. Modern believers with cancer diagnoses or pink slips discover same calm. The world glimpses tranquility and asks for reason; answer: a Person shelters us.

8.6.4 Joy-fueled mission—refugees turned rescuers (2 Cor 5:18–20) Safe people do not hoard shelter; they become ambassadors, pleading "Be reconciled to God." Mission is overflow of astonishment: having received undeserved refuge, they labor to extend banner over enemies. Evangelism thus arises not from guilt trip but from gratitude eruption. Martyrs surrender lives because death only relocates them deeper into refuge. Mercy ministries—food banks, hospitals—are architectural extensions, building on-ramps to gospel stronghold. Joy fuels such construction projects.

8.7 Future Security: From Earthly Stronghold to Eternal City

8.7.1 Perseverance of the saints—kept by divine power (1 Pet 1:5) Peter assures believers they are "guarded by God's power through faith for salvation ready to be revealed." Perseverance is God-energized faith, not self-secured grit. The refuge has no back door; saints may stumble within but cannot wander outside unwittingly. Warning passages serve as railings, keeping pilgrims from cliffs, while Spirit inside inclines them to heed. Eternal security, therefore, motivates endurance, not lethargy.

8.7.2 Glorification: full conformity to the Refuge himself (1 John 3:2) Safety culminates when sequestered sinners become splendid saints, seeing Him as He is and becoming like Him. The refuge then reveals its ultimate purpose: not merely protection **from** wrath but transformation **into** glory. Glorification erases remaining sin residue, ending internal conflict and external decay. Bodies shine like Judge's face once feared, proving that shelter is chrysalis, not coffin.

8.7.3 New-creation dwelling where wrath is past tense (Rev 21:1–4) John's vision describes a city needing no temple because God and Lamb are its light. Tears wiped, death gone, former things passed. Wrath becomes historical footnote, a trophy of justice displayed by nail-prints now ornamenting cosmic peace. Refuge expands into realm; storm dissipates, walls become ornamental gates never shut. Safety shifts from bunker mentality to garden city celebration.

8.7.4 Everlasting worship: the refuge becomes the rejoicing center (Rev 5:9–14) Heaven's liturgy centers on the Lamb who was slain. Songs of deliverance echo eternally, proving shelter itself is stage for adoration. Angels marvel at redemption they never needed; saints sing from experiential gratitude. Worship in eternity never grows dull because every facet of Christ's work reflects infinite beauty. The refuge thus fulfills chief end of humanity: glorifying and enjoying God forever.

8.8 How to Enter and Abide

8.8.1 Repentance-and-faith gate revisited—simplicity and seriousness (Mark 1:15) Entrance requirements remain unchanged since Galilean shoreline: "Repent and believe." No fee, lineage, or ritual prowess necessary. Yet gate is narrow— pride too bulky to squeeze through. Gospel presentations must preserve both simplicity (childlike trust) and seriousness (whole-life surrender). Delayed entry equals tunnel vision amid incoming storm. Evangelists must therefore dismantle complexity without diluting cost.

8.8.2 Means of grace for staying within the walls—Word, sacrament, fellowship Abiding is Spirit-enabled but means-mediated. Daily scripture feeds faith, sacraments renew covenant memory, fellowship supplies exhortation against deceit of sin. Skipping these means resembles neglecting maintenance on lifesaving equipment. Refuge walls do not crack, but negligence may breed self-inflicted misery. Churches function as communal caretakers, distributing nourishment and accountability so all remain rooted.

8.8.3 Battling unbelief: preaching the refuge to oneself daily (Ps 42:5) Psalmist interrogates his downcast soul, commanding hope in God. Self-sermonizing reheats gospel truths, patches leaks of doubt. Believers fight unbelief with promises: "He who did not spare His own Son..." (Rom 8:32). Journaling, singing hymns, and memorizing scripture weaponize mind. The battle continues until glorification; vigilance honors the Builder.

8.8.4 Corporate life in the city of refuge: mutual assurance and discipline Inside the stronghold, citizens practice one-another commands—encourage, admonish, restore. Church discipline rescues wanderers before they drift toward walls' edge. Baptismal vows bind family; Lord's Supper renews covenant. Mutual assurance meetings—testimonies of grace—remind doubters that Builder still works. Thus, abiding is community project; solo Christianity courts danger.

Conclusion

A shelter's quality is measured not by the beauty of its brochures but by its performance in the storm. Christ has already weathered the worst tempest—cosmic wrath—on Good Friday and emerged unscathed on Easter dawn. His person, work, promises, and ongoing ministry form a refuge so comprehensive that nothing—neither death nor life, angels nor demons, present nor future—can penetrate its walls (Rom 8:38–39). Those who have entered may rest secure, yet their security propels them outward to beckon the endangered. Around this refuge the church assembles, her worship echoing like lighthouse beams into night, her fellowship nurturing perseverance until dawn. One day the storm will be history, the refuge will expand into a renewed universe, and the Lamb who once served as storm-shield will stand as sun, flooding every corner with immortal light. Until that unveiling, wise souls will hasten to hide in Christ, abide in Christ, and herald Christ—the sure and only sanctuary for sinners in the hands of a holy God.

Chapter 9. Marks of Genuine Conversion

A seed buried beneath soil is invisible for a season, yet when stalks break the earth and fruit begins to swell the farmer knows that life has truly taken hold (Mark 4 :26-29). In the same way, regeneration is an underground miracle that only God sees in the moment it occurs, but over time it unfailingly pushes sprouts of evidence into the light. The New Testament never imagines a convert who remains unchanged, for the very grace that pardons also "trains us ... to live self-controlled, upright, and godly lives" (Tit 2 :11-12). Assurance, then, is not a mystical hunch; it is the Spirit bearing witness through discernible fruit (Rom 8 :16). These fruits do not earn salvation—just as apples do not create the tree—but they do confirm its species and health. They protect the church from baptizing unbelief, comfort the trembling believer who doubts, and confront the professor whose life betrays the lips (Matt 7 :21-23). The following marks are gathered from the broad witness of Scripture and the distilled wisdom of centuries of pastoral observation. They are not a multiple-choice menu but an integrated portrait of new-creature life. Some traits blossom early and bright, others mature slowly through pruning, yet all will appear in seed form wherever the Spirit has breathed. We begin with the deepest and most foundational evidence: a newly awakened heart toward God himself.

9.1 A New Heart Toward God

The gospel does more than adjust external behavior; it transplants the very core of a person (Ezek 36 :26). The first cluster of evidences, therefore, concerns the believer's changed orientation toward God—his worth, his word, and his will.

9.1.1 Treasuring Christ above all rivals (Phil 3 :7-8)

Paul's testimony—counting "everything as loss because of the surpassing worth of knowing Christ Jesus" (Phil 3 :8)— provides the archetype. Where conversion is genuine, the soul discovers in Christ a beauty and sufficiency that eclipse former idols. Ambitions once tethered to résumé lines or relational conquests begin to loosen, for a superior treasure displaces lesser ones (Matt 13 :44-46). This new valuation system does not destroy earthly joys; it re-orders them beneath the Lord of glory so that gifts are enjoyed without becoming gods (1 Tim 6 :17). Over time, believers notice spontaneous reflexes of praise—songs in traffic jams, thank-yous whispered over simple meals—that were absent before. They feel an ache when Christ is mocked and a pull toward places where he is honored, whether a quiet closet of prayer or a corporate gathering humming with doxology. Such affection can cool under negligence, yet even in seasons of dryness the heart knows where the fountain lies and longs to return. That gravitational re-centering around Jesus, however faint on a given day, is a hallmark no self-reformation can counterfeit.

9.1.2 Ongoing repentance—quick confession and deeper dependence (1 John 1 :9)

Before regeneration, sin either goes unrecognized or is managed by blame-shifting and denial. Afterward, the Spirit sensitizes conscience so that believers run to the light rather than from it (John 3 :20-21). The habit of quick confession—naming the offense without excuse, appealing to the blood of Christ, and rising to new obedience—becomes as regular as spiritual breathing. Far from signalling spiritual failure, this reflex shows a living heart that refuses septic compromise. Over the years repentance also deepens; early on the convert confesses obvious vices, later the Spirit exposes subterranean pride, envy, or prayerlessness. Yet with each layer uncovered, confidence in gospel pardon expands, so humility and joy grow together like twin vines around the same cross. This rhythm of sorrow and hope cannot be faked long-term: legalistic sorrow never escapes self-loathing, antinomian presumption downplays sin, but gospel repentance grieves and rests simultaneously (2 Cor 7 :10-11). Where such reflexive turning persists, the roots of genuine conversion run deep.

9.1.3 Love for God's Word—hunger, submission, and delight (Ps 119 :97)

New birth comes "through the living and abiding word of God" (1 Pet 1 :23); it is unsurprising, then, that the newborn craves the very milk that gave him life (1 Pet 2 :2-3). This craving manifests as a growing appetite to read, hear, and meditate upon Scripture. At first the discipline may feel awkward—like learning to walk—but the underlying hunger keeps the believer returning until familiarity breeds delight. Submission accompanies hunger: difficult texts are wrestled with, not discarded, because the converted heart concedes that the Author is wiser than personal preference. Delight soon follows submission, for obedience uncorks experiential understanding; commands prove sweet once they are tasted (John 7 :17). Over months and years the Bible becomes the lens through which news headlines, family decisions, and personal trials are interpreted. A believer may lapse into seasons of neglect, yet the famine is felt and the table is set again. Persistent indifference to Scripture, however moral one appears, signals an unregenerate palate.

9.1.4 God-centered motives replacing man-pleasing (Gal 1 :10)

Saul of Tarsus once advanced in Judaism partly because he craved the applause of peers; Paul the apostle could later write, "If I were still trying to please man, I would not be a servant of Christ" (Gal 1 :10). Genuine conversion shifts the orientation of the heart from horizontal optics—"What will they think?"—to vertical conscience—"Will this honor my Redeemer?" This does not produce rudeness or social indifference; rather, it liberates the believer to love boldly because reputation is anchored in divine approval. Acts of charity are increasingly performed in secret, prayer gravitates to private rooms, and ethical stands are taken even when costly, because the Father who sees in secret rewards openly (Matt 6 :1-6). This God-centered motive also tempers both pride and despair: praise from others becomes lightweight, criticism loses its paralyzing sting, for identity is fastened to a higher verdict already rendered at the cross. Such reorientation is gradual and often contested, yet its trajectory is unmistakable—a compass needle slowly stabilizing toward true north despite magnetic noise.

9.2 A Transformed Relationship With Sin

Sin once felt like an ally, a familiar rhythm pulsing through desires and decisions. After conversion it becomes an intruder, sometimes still persuasive yet no longer welcome. This altered relationship shows itself in four overlapping ways.

9.2.1 Hatred of formerly cherished idols (Ezek 36 :31)

When the Spirit replaces the heart of stone with living flesh, He also rewires the emotional reflexes attached to transgression. Those reflexes turn from fascination to disgust—"Then you will loathe yourselves for your iniquities" (Ezek 36 :31). The porn habit once defended as "stress relief" now feels like betrayal; gossip that once tasted sweet as dessert now leaves an acrid after-taste. This hatred is visceral as well as rational: the believer can recount specific moments when, mid-temptation, a jolt of revulsion sparked—evidence that a new moral nervous system is online. Such antipathy is rarely instantaneous toward every sin, yet over time it widens its reach, catching not only crude scandals but subtle idolatries such as self-pity or vain comparison. Where affection for known sin persists unchallenged, conversion should be questioned; but where former loves slowly sour, grace is silently at work.

9.2.2 Spirit-enabled warfare—mortifying flesh, vivifying virtue (Rom 8 :13)

Paul's logic is stark: "If by the Spirit you put to death the deeds of the body, you will live" (Rom 8 :13). The phrase *by the Spirit* guards the gospel from two errors. First, moral self-reformation is excluded—flesh cannot kill flesh. Second, passivity is rebuked—the Spirit fights through our yielded efforts, not instead of them. Genuine converts therefore adopt wartime habits: they identify sin-supply lines and cut them (Matt 5 :29-30); they stockpile promise-ammunition by memorizing Scripture (Ps 119 :11); they deploy prayer, accountability, and if necessary professional counsel to press the attack. Victories come with bruises, but the overall campaign advances. The believer who ceases to battle has either forgotten the gospel or never knew its power, for conversion enlists every saint in lifelong insurgency against the flesh.

9.2.3 Observable pattern shift, not sinless perfection (1 John 3 :9-10)

John's assertion that one "born of God does not keep on sinning" troubles tender consciences until context clarifies he speaks of settled, unchecked patterns, not momentary lapses. The tense denotes continuous practice. An unbroken chain of greed, deceit, or impurity reveals unregenerate roots. By contrast, the true Christian's biography shows a before-and-after arc: frequency and intensity of sin decrease, duration of unrepentance shortens, and new virtues sprout. Friends may note a tongue once razor-sharp now learning restraint, a wallet previously clenched now open, a browser history

143

increasingly clean. These unmistakable shifts do not earn heaven; they evidence heaven's life already pulsing within.

9.2.4 Grief over lapses and gospel-anchored recovery (2 Cor 7 :10-11)

Even mature believers stumble, yet their response differs radically from worldly remorse. Godly sorrow owns the offense without minimizing circumstances, drives the sinner back to the cross for cleansing, and produces fresh zeal "to clear yourselves" (2 Cor 7 :11). Shame may whisper withdrawal, but gospel grief runs toward community for prayer and restoration. Over time a pattern emerges: falls become fewer, recoveries faster, humility deeper. The cycle is less like a yo-yo (up-and-down on the same spot) and more like a spiral staircase—sometimes descending steps re-appear, yet in Christ the soul is still ascending overall. Absence of such grief—or wallowing that never reaches faith-filled joy—signals counterfeit conversion or gospel drift.

9.3 Love for the Family of God

New birth inserts believers into a household (Eph 2 :19). Affection for that family is no optional hobby; it is blood-bought instinct.

9.3.1 Covenant commitment to a local church (Acts 2 :41-47)

Pentecost converts were "added" to the Jerusalem assembly, devoting themselves to teaching, fellowship, breaking bread, and prayer. Genuine faith gravitates toward embodied community—not just livestream sermons or solitary podcasts. Membership vows (formal or implicit) declare, *These are my people and I am responsible for them.* Transferable jobs or college relocations prompt diligent search for a new body rather than prolonged independence. Persistent lone-wolf spirituality therefore raises red flags about conversion's authenticity.

9.3.2 Sacrificial service and shared burdens (Gal 6 :2)

Love shows up with rolled-up sleeves. The Spirit prompts believers to shoulder childcare so a weary single mum can worship, to deliver meals to convalescents, to absorb awkwardness in befriending the socially isolated. Financial resources shift too: budgets allocate regular giving, emergency funds become benevolence channels. Such head-heart-hand love fulfills Christ's "new commandment" and validates discipleship (John 13 :34-35).

9.3.3 Peacemaking and quick forgiveness within the body (Eph 4 :32)

Families bicker, but redeemed siblings reconcile quickly. Regenerate hearts lose taste for grudge-nursing, remembering the mountainous debt God forgave them (Matt 18 :21-35). They initiate hard conversations, confess their slice of wrong, and extend grace even before the offender apologizes. Congregations marked by swift forgiveness advertise the gospel more loudly than polished stage lights ever could.

9.3.4 Hospitality that crosses social and ethnic lines (Rom 12 :13)

Jesus is "our peace," creating one new humanity from Jew and Gentile (Eph 2 :14-16). Converted people therefore relish diversity inside the household. Dinner tables become living parables: retirees and college students, immigrants and locals, CEOs and janitors passing bread. Opening one's home—and heart—to those unlike us reveals supernatural affections that society's tribal instincts cannot explain.

9.4 Growth in Practical Holiness

Salvation plants a new root, but that root inevitably presses into visible branches that affect speech, money, sexuality, and vocation. Genuine conversion therefore generates concrete ethical renovation that family members, co-workers, and even casual acquaintances can observe over time.

9.4.1 Tongue tamed—truthful, gracious speech (Jas 3 :2-12)

James likens the tongue to a rudder that steers the whole vessel—small but decisive. Before regeneration, conversation may have been peppered with half-truths, sarcastic jabs, and self-exalting stories. Afterward, the Spirit begins bridling words so that honesty replaces exaggeration, encouragement displaces cynicism, and prayer intrudes where gossip once roamed. This shift is neither instant nor effortless; slips still occur, but they now sting the conscience. Believers ask forgiveness quickly and seek accountability, perhaps inviting a spouse or close friend to flag harmful patterns. Over months, observers notice a gentler tone in family arguments, a refusal to retweet slander online, and a newfound ability to confess weakness without spin. Such verbal fruit cannot grow on the old tree; it signals sap from the Vine.

9.4.2 Financial faithfulness—generosity, integrity, contentment (2 Cor 9 :6-8)

Money once served as scorecard or security blanket, but the gospel redefines it as seed. Those who have received indescribable riches in Christ open their wallets with cheerful eagerness, trusting God's promise of sufficiency and harvest. Tithes are no longer viewed as taxes but as worship; spontaneous gifts to missionaries or struggling saints multiply. Integrity follows: expense reports become accurate, cash-only side jobs get declared, and business practices reject hidden fees. Alongside generosity and honesty blooms contentment—an inner rest that breaks the endless upgrade cycle. Used cars replace debt-laden status vehicles, vacations become opportunities for family ministry, and budget lines appear for almsgiving. Fiscal witnesses like these stun an acquisitive culture and validate the claim that Jesus, not mammon, is Master.

9.4.3 Sexual purity in thought and deed (1 Thess 4 :3-5)

Paul's blunt assertion—"This is the will of God, your sanctification: that you abstain from sexual immorality"—lands with force in every century. The Spirit embarks on a multi-front campaign: internet habits come under scrutiny, flirtatious banter at work is curbed, dating boundaries get tightened, and marital intimacy receives intentional investment. Purity is pursued positively as well—filling imagination with scripture, beauty, and service so that lust finds fewer vacant rooms. Friends install accountability software; singles adopt community-affirmed rhythms; married couples learn to cherish rather than merely coexist. Occasional stumbles drive deeper dependence on grace, but the overarching trajectory is unmistakable: holiness replaces hedonism. A disciple's sexuality becomes a living parable of covenant fidelity, pointing to the ultimate Bridegroom.

9.4.4 Stewardship of time and vocation for God's glory (Col 3 :22-24)

Regenerate hearts realize that every hour and task resides under Christ's lordship. Clock-watching employees transform into diligent workers "serving the Lord, not men." Artists, engineers, and teachers begin to see their craft as worship, pursuing excellence that reflects the Creator's brilliance. Leisure is no longer escapism but restoration and relationship building; endless scrolling gives way to mentoring youth or visiting shut-ins. Calendars gain Sabbath rhythms—weekly rest, daily prayer slots, seasonal retreats—to keep priorities aligned. Career decisions weigh kingdom impact alongside salary, sometimes resulting in radical shifts such as relocating for church planting or downsizing to free bandwidth for foster care. Such stewardship testifies that Christ redeems not only souls but schedules and spreadsheets.

9.5 Enduring Trials With Hope

Conversion does not evacuate believers from hardship; it equips them to pass through fire without losing faith. A storm-tested tree proves its root, and trials reveal whether one's anchor truly holds in Christ.

9.5.1 Joy that co-exists with suffering (1 Pet 1 :6-8)

Peter writes to exiles facing persecution yet describes them as "rejoicing with joy inexpressible." This paradoxical emotion is not denial of pain but simultaneous vision of an imperishable inheritance. New converts may first taste it when initial ridicule from unbelieving friends surprisingly collides with peace rather than resentment. Seasoned saints manifest it at hospital bedsides, singing hymns through tears. Joy's coexistence with sorrow convinces onlookers that something supernatural sustains the sufferer, for stoicism cannot manufacture radiance.

9.5.2 Persevering faith versus temporary enthusiasm (Luke 8 :13-15)

Jesus warned that shallow soil produces rapid sprouts that wither under heat. True conversion, however, embeds roots in gospel depth, enabling endurance when prayers seem unanswered or cultural favor evaporates. Attendance figures fluctuate after scandals or political shifts, yet those truly born of God cling to Christ even if leaders disappoint and programs falter. Their allegiance is to the Shepherd, not the sheep pen. Long-term membership rolls and missionary biographies catalogue such perseverance as silent proof of new life.

9.5.3 Prayerful dependence rather than bitter complaint (Phil 4 :6-7)

Trials squeeze the heart; what spills out reveals its contents. Regenerated hearts instinctively turn anxiety into supplication, presenting requests with thanksgiving. While laments remain brutally honest, they pulse with trust: "Yet I will hope in Him." Bitter cynicism may knock, but disciplined prayer bolts the door, and peace garrisons the mind. Fellowship groups hear testimonies of supernatural calm that passes understanding— even unbelieving doctors notice it in exam rooms.

9.5.4 Refinement of character through affliction (Rom 5 :3-5)

Paul traces a chain: suffering → endurance → proven character → hope. Watch a believer over decades and you'll observe rough edges sanded—impatience mellowing into gentleness, self-reliance bending into empathy. Affliction becomes kiln forging Christ-likeness. Later trials find the saint more pliable, quicker to encourage others because he has "learned the secret" of contentment (Phil 4 :12). This redemptive trajectory distinguishes true grace from mere grit.

9.6 Witness to a Watching World

Grace never contents itself with private piety; it overflows into public testimony that awakens the spiritually comatose and adorns the doctrine of God our Savior (Titus 2 :10). A life reclaimed from wrath is itself a signpost, yet Scripture urges explicit witness that pairs deeds with words.

9.6.1 Verbal testimony of the gospel (Acts 1 :8)

Christ's final promise—"You will be my witnesses"—reaches every genuine convert. The Spirit who illuminates the heart also loosens the tongue. At first, testimony may be halting—a nervous recounting of newfound peace to a sibling—but the impulse is undeniable. Like the Gerasene delivered from demons, believers long to "declare how much God has done" (Luke 8 :39). Courage grows through practice: brief conversations in break rooms, handwritten notes tucked into birthday cards, eventually perhaps teaching roles or street outreach. What distinguishes authentic witness from religious salesmanship is sincerity: a beggar telling another where to find bread, not a quota-driven pitch. Silence in the face of open doors, if habitual and unrepented, suggests either fear quenching the Spirit or the Spirit never having lit the flame. Conversely, regular though imperfect proclamation—tailored to personality and opportunity—confirms that the well inside is truly artesian.

9.6.2 Works of mercy and justice as corroborating evidence (Matt 5 :16)

Jesus insists that good works shine in such a way that onlookers "give glory to your Father." This ethical luminescence verifies the verbal message. Early Christians adopted abandoned infants, scandalizing pagan neighbors; modern disciples volunteer at crisis-pregnancy centers, tutor refugees, or advocate for victims of trafficking. Such deeds are not mere humanitarianism; they are kingdom previews illustrating the character of the King. They also silence slander, for skeptics struggle to dismiss a faith that staffs homeless shelters on winter nights (1 Pet 2 :12). Over time, congregations known for mercy accumulate relational capital that makes evangelistic words credible. Neglect of the poor, by contrast, calls conversion claims into question (1 John 3 :17). Thus hands confirm what lips proclaim, composing a harmonious apologetic.

9.6.3 Cultural distinctness without arrogant separatism (John 17 :14-18)

Christ prayed not for extraction from the world but for protection within it. True converts live as resident aliens— values diverge from prevailing currents, yet compassion keeps them engaged. Their entertainment choices, humor, and spending habits quietly subvert consumerist liturgies. They decline unethical shortcuts at work even when everyone else complies, thereby earning reputations for integrity. Yet they avoid holier-than-thou postures; friendships with unbelievers remain warm, curious, and hospitable. This tension—difference without disdain—baffles observers and invites inquiry. If believers either blend indistinguishably or retreat disdainfully, the salt loses savor. Persistent balance, however awkward at times, signals an internal compass set by heaven.

9.6.4 Burden for the lost expressed in prayer and initiatives (Rom 10 :1)

Paul's heart-cry for Israel models evangelistic anguish. Likewise, regenerate people find their prayer lists increasingly populated by unbelieving relatives, coworkers, and unreached peoples. They fund mission agencies, host international students, or learn new languages to plant churches abroad. Some rearrange retirement plans to spend golden years abroad; others adopt a culture of hospitality so that dinner tables become gospel runways. This expanding circle of concern resists the gravitational pull toward self-absorption. When a professed believer shows chronic apathy toward the destiny of the lost, alarms should sound. Conversely, tears shed in intercession, dollars diverted to mission, and creative outreach ventures all attest that the love of Christ constrains them.

9.7 Submission to Scripture and the Spirit's Leading

A converted heart not only reads the Bible but bows beneath it, and it not only receives the Spirit but follows His promptings. Together, Word and Spirit form the twin rails guiding sanctified discernment.

9.7.1 Doctrinal teachability, rejecting falsehood (John 10 :27)

Jesus' sheep recognize His voice. When confronted with fresh biblical insight—perhaps a hard teaching on forgiveness or a corrective about prosperity myths—the regenerate mind says, "Speak, Lord." This spirit contrasts sharply with unbending self-assurance or chronic suspicion of authority. Teachability does not mean gullibility; believers test every message by Scripture like Bereans (Acts 17 :11). Yet once convinced, they adjust life accordingly. They abandon cherished but unbiblical traditions, submit to church creeds that summarize the apostolic faith, and resist trendy doctrines that tickle ears. Such pliable orthodoxy evidences living faith.

9.7.2 Discernment cultivated by constant practice (Heb 5 :14)

Maturity involves powers of discernment "trained by constant practice to distinguish good from evil." Regenerate believers incrementally develop this skill: weighing entertainment options, detecting manipulative sales tactics, or spotting theological half-truths online. They consult trusted mentors, compare perspectives, and pray for wisdom. Over time, snap judgments better align with Scripture. This moral reflex cannot be downloaded overnight; it grows like muscle through repetitive resistance. Stagnation here—perpetual naivety or cynicism—suggests arrested spiritual development.

9.7.3 Flexibility to Spirit-prompted obedience (Acts 16 :6-10)

Paul's missionary team altered travel plans twice before the Macedonian vision clarified God's route. Likewise, converted people hold dreams loosely, responsive to providential redirection. A spontaneous nudge to encourage a stranger, an unplanned detour to aid a crash victim, or a career pivot sensed after prayer—these illustrate day-to-day guidance. Such flexibility flows from trust: the Shepherd's rod leads to good pastures even when path seems circuitous. Chronic resistance or perpetual second-guessing may expose self-reliance masquerading as prudence; willing responsiveness signals filial confidence.

9.7.4 Harmony of Word and Spirit guarding against extremes (Eph 6 :17)

The sword wielded by the Spirit is expressly "the word of God." Genuine believers therefore refuse to pit pneumatic experience against biblical authority. Visions, impressions, or prophetic words are weighed against Scripture; doctrinal study is warmed by prayerful dependence on the Spirit for illumination. This harmony prevents cold intellectualism on one side and unanchored mysticism on the other. Churches filled with truly converted members exhibit both robust exegesis and vibrant prayer meetings, both catechisms and spiritual gifts pursued decently. Such balance testifies that the same Spirit who inspired the text now indwells the saints.

9.8 Perseverance to the End

Saving faith is not a spark that flickers out when winds rise; it is a Spirit-kindled fire that, though sometimes reduced to embers, can never be extinguished (Phil 1 :6). The hallmark evidence that regeneration is real is its durability under the long pressure of time. Temporary enthusiasm can mimic every prior mark, but it will not survive the marathon (Matt 13 :20-21). Four complementary strands braid together this final sign.

9.8.1 Ongoing faith which God himself sustains (1 Pet 1 :5)

Peter assures beleaguered exiles that they "are being guarded by God's power through faith for a salvation ready to be revealed." The grammar is staggering: God's omnipotence keeps the saint, yet the channel is the believer's own faith—an active, conscious reliance that refuses to relinquish Christ. Genuine converts therefore continue, however falteringly, to say "Amen" to the gospel every day. Intellectual assaults may raise questions, moral failures may cloud assurance, physical decline may tax emotions, yet beneath each wave the Spirit keeps buoyant trust. Seasons of doubt come, but apostasy does not. When Peter faltered, Christ's intercession guaranteed that his faith would not fail utterly (Luke 22 :32). The very presence of embattled yet persistent trust, sometimes reduced to a whisper—"Lord, to whom shall we go?" (John 6 :68)—is proof that the same God who authored faith continues to uphold it.

9.8.2 Corporate safeguards—discipline and encouragement (Heb 3 :13)

Perseverance is a community project. The writer of Hebrews commands believers to exhort one another "every day ... that none of you may be hardened by the deceitfulness of sin." Mutual counsel, confession, and accountability operate like guardrails on a mountain road, preventing sleepy travelers from plunging over cliffs. Formal church discipline serves as the extreme version of that guardrail, shocking a professing believer to awaken and return while there is still time (1 Cor

5 :4-5). At the other pole, simple encouragement—texts, meals, shared psalms—puts courage back into sagging hearts. True converts welcome, even invite, such intrusions because they fear sin's subtlety more than brotherly rebuke. Chronic isolation or hostility toward loving correction is therefore a danger signal that perseverance may be a façade masking unbelief.

9.8.3 Finishing well—examples and exhortations (2 Tim 4 :7-8)

Paul, staring at imminent execution, could testify, "I have fought the good fight ... I have kept the faith." Scripture scatters similar finish-line portraits—Joseph enduring palace and prison, Caleb still conquering mountains at eighty-five, Anna praying into her nineties. These stories exhort younger saints to build habits that age gracefully: daily Scripture intake, confessing sin quickly, maintaining soft hearts toward correction. They also comfort the elderly convert who wonders if late-life frailty disqualifies usefulness; God counts clinging faith, not physical stamina, as victory. Conversely, Scripture warns by negative example—Demas loving the present world (2 Tim 4 :10), the wilderness generation falling short (Heb 3 :16-19). Genuine believers tremble at such warnings and lean harder into grace, proving the warnings effective means of perseverance rather than predictions of collapse.

9.8.4 Eschatological orientation—living for "that Day" (2 Pet 3 :11-14)

Peter asks, "What sort of people ought you to be in lives of holiness and godliness, waiting for and hastening the coming of the day of God?" Hope fixed on the return of Christ functions like a magnet pulling the pilgrim forward. It relativizes today's pains and today's pleasures, freeing the saint to take courageous risks—overseas missions, counter-cultural generosity, integrity that could cost a promotion—because any loss will be eclipsed by resurrection glory (Rom 8 :18). Daily decisions begin to smell of eternity: investments weighed by kingdom yield, conversations salted with everlasting stakes. When the crown of righteousness is prized above likes, followers, or quarterly returns, perseverance gains practical traction. A believer who ceases to look for the blessed hope will soon drift; one who keeps the telescope of faith trained on the horizon will finish the race with eyes lifted.

Conclusion

An apple tree need not strain to produce apples; life within naturally expresses itself in fruit without. Likewise, the new birth inevitably reveals its reality through transformed affections, behaviors, relationships, and endurance. These marks do not inflate the believer's résumé before God—they spotlight the Redeemer's power before the world. When examined together, they offer the trembling child of God a solid ground for assurance while exposing the hollow shell of empty profession. May every reader submit humbly to this scriptural mirror, rejoicing wherever even the smallest buds of grace appear, and hastening to Christ for pardon and power where barrenness is uncovered. For on the last day, no counterfeit leaves, no fruitless branch, will stand. Only those whose lives bear the signature of the Spirit will hear the Master's voice: "Well done, good and faithful servant ... enter into the joy of your Lord" (Matt 25 :23).

Chapter 10. Living Under Grace Yet Aware of Wrath

Grace and wrath are not alternate moods in God's heart; they are complementary facets of His single, undivided holiness. Grace is holiness moving toward the sinner in costly love; wrath is holiness standing against sin in unflinching justice. A believer who loses sight of either facet will limp through discipleship—legalism looms when wrath eclipses grace, licentious presumption festers when grace is severed from wrath. The New Testament insists that mature Christians keep both truths in steady tension. Paul exults that "there is therefore now no condemnation for those who are in Christ Jesus" (Rom 8:1) yet warns the same church that "each of us will give an account of himself to God" (Rom 14:12). The writer to the Hebrews crowns a radiant discourse on the new covenant with the thunderous reminder: "Our God is a consuming fire" (Heb 12:29). Genuine gospel equilibrium produces worship that both sings and trembles, ethics fueled by gratitude yet braced with sober vigilance, and witness that woos prodigals while awakening sleepers. This chapter traces that equilibrium from biblical foundations into every arena of daily life so that redeemed people may walk the narrow ridge—secure beneath Calvary's banner yet sensitized to the smoke of approaching judgment—for their own joy and the world's good.

10.1 The Grace-Wrath Dialectic in Scripture

10.1.1 Psalmist paradox—"steadfast love" and "consuming fire" in one stanza

The Psalms refuse simplistic portraits of God. David can celebrate covenant mercy in one breath—"The steadfast love of the LORD is from everlasting to everlasting on those who fear Him" (Ps 103:17)—and in the next warn that the same LORD "will rain coals on the wicked" (Ps 11:6). This lyrical tension trains the worshiper's imagination to embrace complexity rather than choose a half-truth. Steadfast love (*hesed*) is pictured as mother-like tenderness encircling covenant children, while wrath is depicted as a furnace melting mountain ranges (Ps 97:3-5). Neither cancels the other; both spring from divine holiness, like twin streams diverging around a great rock. Israel's history confirms the paradox: the God who bore His people on eagle's wings at the Red Sea later scorched their presumption with fiery serpents (Num 21:6). The psalmists do not apologize for the tension; they harness it to deepen awe, persuade the presumptuous to repent, and comfort the oppressed that evil will not stand unopposed. Modern Christians who chant only love-infused choruses or only judgment-laden laments truncate the biblical soundtrack and impoverish their souls.

10.1.2 Calvary as simultaneous display of mercy and vengeance (Rom 3:25-26)

The cross is not God's apology for Old-Testament severity; it is the blazing intersection where severity and mercy embrace without compromise. Paul declares that God "put [Christ]

157

forward as a propitiation by His blood ... to show His righteousness" so that He might be "just and the justifier" of the ungodly (Rom 3:25-26). Justice is upheld because sin is punished in the substitute; mercy triumphs because the substitute is God's own Son. Thus the very place believers sing "amazing grace" is also the place they glimpse wrath concentrated like sunlight through a magnifying lens. Every communion cup therefore contains twin reminders: crimson life poured out so guilt is erased, and cruciform warning that the Judge does not sweep iniquity under a cosmic rug. Contemplation of Calvary should foster tears of gratitude and chills of reverence in the same heartbeat. A gospel that blunts the edge of divine vengeance hollows out the glory of mercy, for grace tastes sweetest against the bitter backdrop of what it cost.

10.1.3 Eschatological tension—already justified, not yet escaped Bema evaluation (2 Cor 5:10)

Justification pronounces the believer righteous once for all, yet Scripture still speaks of a future tribunal where each work is weighed. Paul reminds the Corinthian church—secure in Christ—that "we must all appear before the judgment seat (bēma) of Christ" to receive what is due for deeds done in the body (2 Cor 5:10). This assessment is not to decide heaven or hell—that issue was settled when Christ's righteousness was imputed—but to evaluate faithfulness and assign rewards or loss (1 Cor 3:12-15). Living under grace, therefore, does not dissolve accountability; it reorients it. Good works become thank-offerings that delight the Father and will be celebrated openly, while neglected stewardship still matters and may forfeit eternal commendation. Far from breeding anxiety, this prospect energizes perseverance, for the Judge is also the Savior who enables the very obedience He will later praise (Phil 2:12-13). Yet the warning note safeguards against complacency: to squander grace is real tragedy. The healthy heart can say with Luther, "We are saved by faith alone, but the faith that saves is never alone."

10.1.4 Apostolic warnings as means of preserving heirs (Col 1:22-23)

Paul announces that Christ has reconciled believers "in His body of flesh by His death" in order to present them holy—*if* they continue in the faith, stable and steadfast (Col 1:22-23). The conditional clause is not a crack in the foundation of security but the God-ordained instrument by which He keeps His children alert. Warnings function like guardrails on a mountain pass: true pilgrims heed them and stay on the road, false disciples ignore them and plummet. Peter employs the same strategy, urging saints to be diligent lest they fall from steadfastness (2 Pet 3:17). Thus, living under grace does not mean muting admonitions; it means recognizing them as expressions of fatherly love. Parents secure toddlers with firm words near a cliff not because love is uncertain, but because protection expresses love. So, too, the Spirit uses Scripture's warnings to awaken drowsy consciences, steer saints back to the path, and in the process fulfill Jesus' promise that none whom the Father has given Him will perish (John 6:39).

10.2 Worship That Trembles and Sings

10.2.1 Reverence: recovering godly fear in liturgy (Heb 12 :28)

The writer of Hebrews instructs believers to "offer to God acceptable worship, with reverence and awe, for our God is a consuming fire" (Heb 12 :28-29). Genuine Christian liturgy therefore refuses both frivolous levity and paralyzing dread. Reverence begins in the pulpit as pastors unfold texts that reveal divine majesty, but it is carried by the entire congregation: arriving punctually out of respect, preparing hearts in silent prayer, and participating with alert minds rather than passive observation. Architecture, music, and posture can all serve reverence—a brief moment of kneeling or a quiet instrumental interlude invites reflection on holiness. Yet reverence is chiefly an interior bowing: an awareness that the One addressed flung galaxies into orbit and once shook Sinai until rocks cracked. When that consciousness pervades a service, even children sense gravity. No one leaves asking, "Was it fun?" but rather, "Did we meet with the Lord?"

10.2.2 Joyful exultation grounded in un-shakeable acceptance (Rom 5 :1-2)

Grace, however, does more than hush us—it lifts our heads. Justified by faith, "we have peace with God ... and rejoice in hope of the glory of God" (Rom 5 :1-2). Worship that omits jubilation dishonors the gospel as surely as worship that omits awe. Corporate singing should therefore move from confession to celebration, mirroring Psalm 32 where forgiven David shouts for joy. Testimonies of conversion and baptism sprinkle the assembly with fresh wonder. The preacher who has faithfully wounded consciences with law must then heal them with Christ's finished work, sending saints out singing louder than when they entered. Holy joy is not emotional hype; it is blood-bought confidence that wrath is passed and favor abides. When reverence and rejoicing intertwine, worshipers taste the very equilibrium this chapter commends.

10.2.3 Songs, prayers, and Scripture readings that keep both accents in harmony

A thoughtful liturgy curates content so that wrath and grace mingle rather than compete. Consider opening with a call to worship from Psalm 95, which first invites praise and then warns not to harden hearts. Follow confession of sin with an assurance of pardon from 1 John 1 :9, then sing a hymn that celebrates rescue—"And can it be that I should gain?" Pastoral prayers include lament for societal evil (wrath remembered) and thanksgiving for adoption (grace savored). Scripture readings move from Exodus plague narratives to Romans 8 victory. Such weaving trains congregations over months to inhabit the full biblical rhythm. Neglecting either thread distorts the tapestry: all wrath turns services into courtrooms without closing benediction; all grace produces pep rallies lacking moral gravity. Balanced curation teaches hearts to hold both notes Monday through Saturday.

10.2.4 Communion as weekly rehearsal of wrath averted and grace enjoyed

The Lord's Table embodies the paradox: the broken bread proclaims judgment executed; the shared cup celebrates covenant welcome. Regular frequency—weekly or monthly—engrains this dual remembrance. Self-examination (1 Cor 11 :28) preserves sobriety, yet the invitation—"Take, eat"—radiates hospitality. Silence while elements are distributed allows saints to ponder the cosmic transaction; corporate singing during distribution lets joy overflow. Children observing sense both the seriousness of spilling blood and the warmth of family supper. Thus the sacrament tutors the community in simultaneous trembling and singing better than a thousand lectures.

10.3 Holiness Fueled by Gratitude and Sobriety

10.3.1 Gratitude-driven obedience: love that keeps commandments (John 14 :15)

Jesus links affection and action: "If you love me, you will keep my commandments." Gratitude for blood-bought pardon becomes energy for daily choices. The believer resists pornography not merely to avoid guilt but to honor the Bridegroom who died to present a pure bride. He forgives enemies because he recalls his own canceled ledger (Eph 4 :32). Gratitude shifts holiness from grim duty to glad allegiance. Yet emotion alone wobbles; therefore the mind daily rehearses specific gospel benefits—adoption, intercession, promised inheritance—fueling the heart's furnace for fresh obedience.

10.3.2 Sobriety against relapse: remembering Lot's wife (Luke 17 :32)

Jesus' terse command—"Remember Lot's wife"—injects holy caution. She escaped physical Sodom but not its gravitational pull on her heart. Christians under grace still carry fleshly residue; vigilance is required lest old cravings regain throne. Sobriety expresses itself in watchfulness over media intake, friendships, and schedule fatigue that weakens resistance. Community groups ask hard questions; elders model transparent repentance. Rather than contradicting assurance, such caution protects it, just as guardrails protect scenic mountain drives.

10.3.3 Spiritual disciplines that celebrate adoption yet mortify the flesh (Rom 8 :12-17)

Prayer, fasting, Scripture meditation, and journaling are not payments but pipelines—means for the Spirit to testify adoption and simultaneously slay sinful impulses. Fasting exposes hidden dependencies; Scripture memorization replaces lies with truth; Sabbath rest proclaims trust in Fatherly provision. Each practice is framed by identity ("Abba, Father") while fighting residual rebellion ("Put to death the deeds of the body"). The healthiest rule of life thus weds celebration and mortification in one routine rhythm.

10.3.4 Accountability structures balancing encouragement and admonition

Peer discipleship flourishes when members give both hugs and warnings. Meetings begin with sharing evidences of grace—celebrating growth—then pivot to probing challenges. Leaders cultivate atmospheres where confessing relapse receives empathy and a plan, not shock and gossip. Scripture's dual note shapes tone: Galatians 6 :1 restores gently (grace), yet Hebrews 3 :13 exhorts lest any be hardened (wrath awareness). Where groups drift into mere therapy or, conversely, rigid inspection, the gospel equilibrium has tilted. Balanced accountability sustains long-haul holiness.

10.4 Pastoral Care in a Grace-and-Wrath Framework

10.4.1 Counseling the anxious—assurance without antinomian laxity

Some souls, haunted by sensitive consciences, fear they have out-sinned grace. Pastors apply promises like Romans 8 :1, tracing substitution in detail until peace settles. Yet they also guard against turning assurance into license, clarifying that the same cross that cancels guilt also claims allegiance (1 Cor 6 :19-20). Homework may include writing a gratitude list and planning concrete obedience steps, displaying the inseparability of acceptance and transformation.

10.4.2 Addressing the complacent—lawful warnings without legalistic despair

Other sheep bask in cheap grace, presuming on security while courting sin. Here pastors deploy warnings: "Those who live according to the flesh will die" (Rom 8 :13). They recount Lot's wife, Ananias and Sapphira, and Hebrews 10 :26-27. Yet each warning is tethered to hope—repentance is still open, the Spirit still empowers change. The aim is conviction leading to restoration, not condemnation driving to despair. This surgical use of terror and tenderness imitates Paul's "knowing the fear of the Lord, we persuade others" (2 Cor 5 :11).

10.4.3 Church discipline as loving guardrail, not punitive exile (Matt 18 :15-17)

When private admonitions fail, the church escalates for the sinner's rescue. Excommunication removes false assurance by treating the person as outside the covenant, hoping godly sorrow will awaken repentance (1 Cor 5 5). The congregation mourns but does not vilify, remembering that restoration is the goal (2 Cor 2 :6-8). Discipline therefore embodies both wrath awareness (sin endangers eternally) and grace hope (repentance restores fully).

10.4.4 Funeral liturgies: celebrating grace while preaching eternity's stakes

Christian funerals must comfort mourners with gospel hope— "absent from the body, present with the Lord"—yet also remind the living that judgment awaits. Eulogies include honest acknowledgment of the deceased's faith fruit, not canonization; Scripture readings like 1 Thess 4 :13-18 and Matt 25 :31-46 frame the loss in eschatological light. Unbelieving attendees hear both invitation and warning. Thus funerals become evangelistic platforms where grace and wrath mingle with tears and hallelujahs.

10.5 Family and Vocational Life in Light of Dual Realities

10.5.1 Parenting disciples: teaching children delight and dread (Eph 6 :4)

Grace-aware parents resist the twin errors of permissive "buddy-parenting" and fear-based authoritarianism. Paul commands fathers to raise children "in the discipline and instruction of the Lord," a phrase that mingles nurture with warning. Practical obedience means explaining gospel truths early—why Jesus had to face God's wrath—and celebrating them often through story Bibles, catechism songs, and answered-prayer journals. It also means enforcing boundaries consistently so that children connect disobedience with consequences, a miniature picture of the moral universe. Mealtime prayers rehearse both gratitude for undeserved kindness and sobriety about a world where sin still destroys. When discipline is required, the cross shapes tone: firm yet restorative, always pointing to the Savior who bore punishment in our place. Over years, sons and daughters learn to tremble at God's holiness while running to His open arms—a posture they will need long after they leave the nest.

10.5.2 Marriage mirrors—extending grace yet honoring holy boundaries

Husbands and wives who know they were rescued from wrath cannot demand perfection from each other; forgiveness becomes the marital language (Col 3 :13). At the same time, grace never excuses toxic patterns—abuse, addiction, secret sin; the covenant's holiness requires intervention, counsel, and sometimes church discipline. Regular confession and prayer together anchor the couple in shared dependence, turning conflict into an altar rather than a courtroom. Date nights commemorate kindnesses of God, strengthening joy, while scheduled "state-of-the-union" talks surface small resentments before they metastasize. Sexual intimacy is stewarded as a covenant celebration, guarded against pornography precisely because wrath fell on impurity at Calvary (Heb 13 :4). Financial decisions weigh generosity and stewardship, modeling for children that treasure lies beyond this age. Thus the marriage covenant becomes a living parable—stern in loyalty, lavish in mercy—reflecting the gospel it proclaims.

10.5.3 Marketplace ethics under the eye of gracious yet judging Lord (Col 3 :22-25)

Employees mindful of future judgment work "not with eye-service, as people-pleasers, but with sincerity of heart, fearing the Lord." They refuse to inflate invoices, fudge mileage reports, or manipulate metrics because every spreadsheet cell lies open before Christ. Grace fuels excellence: jobs become altars of gratitude where talents are returned to their Giver. For employers, wrath awareness deters exploitation of labor or shady environmental shortcuts; grace compels generous wages, mentoring, and second-chance hiring. Believers mark promotions with thanksgiving offerings and handle layoffs with transparent compassion. When ethical stands cost advancement, they remember that any earthly loss counts "not worthy to be compared" with the glory ahead (Rom 8 :18). Colleagues may not parse theology, but they notice integrity under pressure and ask for the hope that explains it.

10.5.4 Stewardship of time and money as gratitude response and judgment preparation

Grace rescues calendars and budgets from entropy. Disciples schedule personal devotions and corporate worship first, trusting God to multiply remaining hours. They view savings not as hoarded security but seed for future kingdom generosity; retirement portfolios become mission vehicles rather than pleasure stockpiles. Annual reviews invite the Spirit's audit: Have I invested talents in light of the Master's return (Matt 25 :14-30)? Sabbath practices—digital fasts, unhurried meals, nature walks—preach freedom from frantic self-importance. Charitable giving targets both mercy ministries (relieving present suffering) and gospel proclamation (averting eternal wrath), demonstrating holistic love. By budgeting to bless unseen generations—Bible translations, foster-care scholarships—saints send treasure ahead where moth and rust can't devour (Matt 6 :19-21). In all, time and money serve as visible timers counting down to the day when accounts close and joy begins.

10.6 Public Witness: Mercy Offerings and Warning Trumpets

10.6.1 Evangelism that invites prodigals and cautions rebels (Acts 17 :30-31)

Paul's Areopagus sermon models dual tone: he announces universal commands to repent and a fixed day of judgment while offering proof through resurrection. Modern heralds likewise blend warmth—sharing coffee, listening to stories—with frank talk about wrath to come. Tracts and testimonies highlight both ransom and reckoning, avoiding the bait-and-switch of "God loves you" without context. Street evangelists include pleas like "flee the coming wrath," but conclude with "come home—the Father runs to meet you." Churches host seeker forums where hard questions meet thoughtful apologetics grounded in holiness. Follow-up discipleship emphasizes assurance early so that converts share faith naturally. Over time, neighborhoods feel the pulse of a community both compassionate and candid.

10.6.2 Social justice pursued with eschatological gravitas (Jas 5 :1-5)

James warns wealthy oppressors that unpaid wages cry to heaven; Christians hear that echo and advocate for fair labor laws, anti-trafficking reforms, and racial equity. Yet they do so without utopian naïveté, knowing only Christ's return completes justice. This eschatological realism sustains long-haul activism when legislation stalls. Protest signs read "Love your neighbor" on one side and "Prepare to meet your God" on the other. Mercy ministries pair food banks with gospel conversations, treating bodies and souls inseparably. Believers lament systemic sin publicly, confessing complicity, while refusing to cancel offenders—offering repentance pathways instead. Such balanced engagement confounds political categories, showcasing a kingdom not of this world yet deeply for this world.

10.6.3 Apologetics appealing to conscience and highlighting accountability (Rom 2 :15-16)

Human hearts carry moral law inked on conscience. Effective defenders of the faith press that awareness, asking skeptics why injustice outrages them or beauty moves them if the universe is aimless. They expose borrowed capital when critics demand fairness yet deny transcendent standards. Arguments climax in the risen Judge who will "judge the secrets of men" (Rom 2 :16). Still, apologists season truth with gentleness, remembering they too were under wrath. Debates end with invitation, not humiliation, keeping door to refuge open.

10.6.4 Civic engagement—salt and light without utopian illusions

Christians vote, lobby, and serve in public office aware that governments are ordained yet provisional. They resist both

167

withdrawal (ceding culture to decay) and idolatry (equating partisan victory with kingdom come). Policy positions flow from love of neighbor and respect for divine moral order; tone remains respectful because rulers are God's servants (Rom 13 :1-7). When legislative wins occur, believers give thanks but stay vigilant, knowing laws can restrain sin but not regenerate hearts. When losses mount, they lament without despair, trusting a city whose builder is God (Heb 11 :10). In all, their presence preserves societal conscience like salt delaying rot while shining gospel light into dark halls.

10.7 Spiritual Warfare and Eschatological Vigilance

10.7.1 Armored by grace, alert to wrath-deserving schemes (Eph 6 :10-18)

Paul's armor passage roots every piece in gospel truth: righteousness, readiness from the gospel of peace, salvation helmet. Believers therefore fight not for victory but from it. Yet warfare is real—cosmic powers whisper lies that minimize sin or distort grace. Daily prayer straps on armor: rehearsing justification cuffs breastplate, meditating on adoption tightens helmet straps. Awareness that wrath nearly fell on them before Christ keeps soldiers humble, not haughty. They rescue captives gently, mindful of former bondage (2 Tim 2 :24-26).

10.7.2 Prayer as front-line watchfulness (Mark 13 :33)

Jesus' end-time discourse closes with "Stay awake." Prayer is the eyelid of the soul—when it droops, temptation slips. Churches schedule monthly vigils, praying for revival, justice, and perseverance. Families adopt morning or bedtime intercession routines, teaching kids to see news headlines as prompts rather than noise. Personal "Nehemiah prayers" (quick arrow-requests during work) keep awareness of God amid deadlines. Such vigilance doesn't breed paranoia; it nurtures expectancy—lamps trimmed, oil stocked.

10.7.3 Discernment of false teachers who mute wrath or muffle grace (2 Pet 2 :1-3)

Peter warns of swindlers who exploit with "destructive heresies." Some downplay judgment, promising peace to unrepentant hearts; others smother grace under law-keeping burdens. Wise congregations examine sermons: Does this message exalt Christ's cross and warn of sin's wages? Book clubs vet bestsellers, accepting gems and rejecting poisons. Social-media prophets face Berean scrutiny before shares. Elders publish doctrinal statement updates, equipping saints to spot errors. Protection here is pastoral love, not gatekeeping pride.

10.7.4 Perseverance through trials as demonstration of balanced hope (1 Thess 1 :9-10)

Thessalonians turned from idols "to wait for His Son ... who delivers us from the wrath to come." Their patience amid persecution evidenced genuine conversion. Modern parallels include believers refusing to renounce Christ under workplace pressure, students enduring ridicule for chastity, seniors praising God in hospice beds. Their hope is not escapism but expectant realism: wrath will end evil, grace will crown faithfulness. Observers often convert after witnessing such durable joy, proving that balanced hope evangelizes even without words.

Conclusion

To live under grace yet aware of wrath is to inhale and exhale with both lungs of the gospel. Inhaling, we breathe assurance—no condemnation, full adoption, unbreakable promises. Exhaling, we release reverent awe—holy fear that keeps us vigilant, humble, and urgent for a perishing world. Cut off either breath and spiritual life atrophies; keep both and the church strides forward with steady heartbeat. May every reader cultivate this sacred rhythm: tremble, then sing; rest, then run; adore the Lamb who bore wrath, and announce the Lion who will roar in judgment. For the day is near when faith becomes sight, mercy crowns the faithful, and wrath removes every rival glory so that grace may fill the universe forever.

Chapter 11. Preaching Terror, Offering Mercy

Jonathan Edwards delivered *Sinners in the Hands of an Angry God* in the summer of 1741, and the congregation at Enfield reportedly grasped their pew rails in terror as the invisible floor of divine patience seemed to crack beneath their souls. Yet the same sermon glimmered with gospel promise— "and now you have an extraordinary opportunity, a day wherein Christ has flung the door of mercy wide open." Edwards was not being paradoxical; he was being biblically balanced. From the first warning in Eden ("in the day you eat... you shall surely die," Gen 2 :17) to the final invitation of Revelation ("let the one who is thirsty come," Rev 22 :17), Scripture marries terrifying judgment to tender mercy. Preachers who would speak for God must sound both notes or they will misrepresent His character, deform the church's worship, and imperil their hearers' souls. Our cultural moment—therapeutic, easily offended, allergic to authority— tempts heralds to whisper about wrath or, in some circles, to thunder without tears. This chapter contends that faithful proclamation requires the two-edged trumpet of law and gospel, terror and mercy, severity and kindness (Rom 11 :22). We will trace the biblical mandate for that dual note, dissect the anatomy of awakening sermons, examine rhetorical and pastoral strategies, and consider how such preaching travels across generations. The goal is not homiletical technique alone but the salvation and sanctification of immortal souls. As Richard Baxter urged, we must preach as dying men to dying men, yet also as pardoned rebels offering the King's own invitation to His banquet hall.

11.1 The Biblical Mandate for Warning and Invitation

11.1.1 Old-Testament watchmen: Ezekiel's blood-on-the-hands commission (Ezek 3 :17-19)

Yahweh appoints Ezekiel a "watchman for the house of Israel," stationing him on the wall to spot approaching judgment. If the prophet fails to sound the trumpet, the wicked man will perish—but God will "require his blood at your hand" (Ezek 3 :18). Conversely, if Ezekiel warns and the hearer ignores, the sentinel is guilt-free. This commission establishes a two-fold responsibility: proclamation and persuasion. Silence in the face of sin is complicity; speech divorced from compassion is cruelty. The pattern recurs in Isaiah's watchmen (Isa 62 :6-7) and Jeremiah's weeping laments (Jer 9 :1-3). The covenant community learns that divine love provides advance notice, and divine justice holds messengers accountable for muzzled truth. Modern preachers stand in that lineage: withholding the reality of hell is not kindness but spiritual malpractice that stains the conscience with innocent blood.

11.1.2 John the Baptist and Jesus: ax-at-the-root, yoke-that-is-easy (Matt 3 :10; 11 :28-30)

John's desert cry splits the quiet of four hundred prophetic years: "Even now the axe is laid to the root of the trees" (Matt

172

3 :10). Crowds sense the blade and ask, "What then shall we do?" (Luke 3 :10-14). Yet the same herald points to the Lamb who removes sin (John 1 :29). Jesus continues the rhythm: warning cities of hotter Gehenna than Sodom (Matt 11 :20-24) while beckoning the weary to a gentle yoke (Matt 11 :28-30). His fiercest denunciations (Matt 23) flow from wounded love that would gather Jerusalem under protective wings (Matt 23 :37). Law and gospel, threat and promise, operate like chest compressions and rescue breaths in spiritual resuscitation. Any ministry claiming Christ's mantle must wield both: the scalpel of conviction and the balm of grace.

11.1.3 Apostolic precedent—"knowing the fear ... we persuade" (2 Cor 5 :11)

Paul surveys the cosmic courtroom—"we must all appear before the judgment seat of Christ" (2 Cor 5 :10)—and draws a missionary conclusion: "Therefore, knowing the fear of the Lord, we persuade others" (v. 11). Fear here is not paralyzing dread but sober awareness that propels persuasive effort. His sermons in Acts mirror that blend: at Pisidian Antioch he warns that scoffers will perish (Acts 13 :40-41) and immediately offers forgiveness through the risen Savior (vv. 38-39). Felix trembles when Paul reasons about righteousness and judgment (Acts 24 :25), yet the apostle also speaks of "faith in Christ Jesus" (v. 24). Peter, too, couples indictment ("you crucified") with invitation ("repent and be baptized...for the forgiveness of sins," Acts 2 :23-39). Thus New-Testament preaching is structurally bipolar—law first, then gospel; death sentence, then pardon. Departing from this order de-formats apostolic proclamation.

11.1.4 Theological engine: holiness, justice, and covenant mercy converging at Calvary

Behind the biblical mandate lies God's immutable character. Holiness demands separation from sin (Isa 6 :3-5); justice requires retribution (Rom 6 :23); covenant love longs to forgive (Ex 34 :6-7). At Calvary these attributes converge without dilution. Wrath is not suppressed but satisfied in the sin-bearing Substitute (Gal 3 :13). Mercy triumphs by means of wrath borne, not bypassed (Rom 3 :25-26). Therefore preaching that isolates love from justice mis-portrays the cross, like displaying a diamond without its dark velvet backdrop. Conversely, preaching wrath without grace denies the very purpose for which Jesus was given. Theology thus fuels homiletics: a full-orbed gospel requires the preacher to thunder and to whisper, to expose guilt and extol grace, because God Himself is both light unapproachable and Father of mercies (1 Tim 6 :16; 2 Cor 1 :3).

11.2 Anatomy of a Soul-Awakening Sermon

11.2.1 Text selection that exposes sin and unveils the Savior

A sermon meant to rouse sleepers must spring from a passage that does both halves of gospel work: it must reveal humanity's peril and God's provision. That usually means choosing pericopes where law and grace stand in deliberate tension—Nathan's parable followed by David's pardon (2 Sam 12 :1-13), Isaiah's temple vision joined to the coal of atonement (Isa 6 :1-7), or Paul's Galatian indictment flowing into cruciform justification (Gal 3). The expositor resists plucking isolated "hell verses" or "comfort verses" that flatten Scripture's dramatic arc; instead, he allows the inspired text to set the sermonic thermostat. Careful exegesis situates warnings in their covenant context so hearers sense God's holy consistency rather than capricious anger. Likewise, gospel promises are traced to their Christological fulfillment, preventing moralism. When the congregation sees wrath arise organically from the passage and mercy crest on the same wave, they grasp that the preacher is not manipulating emotions but letting God speak. Such alignment builds credibility, disarms defensiveness, and invites Spirit-wrought conviction.

11.2.2 Exegetical honesty: letting the passage set the temperature

After choosing the text, the preacher must submit to it emotionally as well as intellectually. If the passage blazes with judgment—Amos' roar against Samaria or Jesus' woes on Chorazin—the sermon must not shrink to a lukewarm chat lest it mute divine passion. Conversely, when the Scripture overflows with consolation—Psalm 103 or Romans 8—the tone must swell with matching comfort, not remain stuck in thunder mode. Exegetical honesty also means admitting hard edges: hell is eternal (Matt 25 :46), wrath is personal (Rom 1 :18), and grace is undeserved (Eph 2 :8-9). Glossing over difficulties to maintain audience approval betrays the text and inoculates sinners against true repentance. Quoting feared verses verbatim, explaining original-language nuances, and illustrating context keep God's voice dominant over the preacher's preferences. Listeners learn that Scripture, not sentiment, wields authority; therefore their quarrel is with God, not merely the messenger. Such fidelity, even when uncomfortable, fertilizes lasting fruit.

11.2.3 Classical gospel order—law that wounds, gospel that heals

Historic evangelicals recognized an order to spiritual surgery: first the scalpel, then the suture. Edwards, Whitefield, Spurgeon, and Lloyd-Jones all employed this "law–gospel" architecture. The law section defines sin, displays holiness, and dismantles self-righteous refuge, often using specific indictments (pride, greed, lust) so consciences cannot abstract the charges. Illustrations here cut close to daily life—tax fraud, porn clicks, ethnic prejudice—until hearers feel exposed. Once the Spirit has laid the heart bare, the preacher pivots to Christ crucified, risen, and willing, pouring balm on fresh wounds. Timing matters: premature comfort leaves the tumor; prolonged wounding produces despair. Transition sentences—"But there is a fountain..."—signal the gospel turn. The cure is proclaimed with equal specificity: substitution for lustful hearts, adoption for orphans of shame, Spirit power for enslaved wills. Listeners then see that the severity of diagnosis matches the magnificence of cure; many bow in wonder.

11.2.4 Imagery, analogy, and narrative: painting eternity on the listener's imagination

Prose alone seldom penetrates modern attention spans dulled by screens; vivid imagery grabs the affections. Edwards likened sinners to a spider dangling above flames. Spurgeon pictured unconverted churchgoers sleeping on a mast amid stormy seas. Such metaphors translate abstract doctrine into mental movies viewers replay long after the benediction. The preacher mines biblical images—worm that dies not, city of refuge, marriage feast—and updates them with contemporary equivalents: a levee about to break, a bank alert flashing "insufficient funds." Narrative does similar work: a current news story of corporate fraud can illustrate hidden sin exposed; a rescue-at-sea headline can foreshadow gospel deliverance. Analogies must remain subordinate to exegesis, lest creativity eclipse truth, but when yoked well they stir holy emotions. Aim for concrete senses—sounds of collapsing beams, acrid smoke of judgment, warm embrace of the Father—so eternity feels near and urgent.

11.3 Rhetorical Strategies for Shaking the Self-Assured

11.3.1 Vivid portrayals of peril without theatrical gimmickry

Authentic gravity differs from spectacle. The preacher need not dim lights, cue thunder audio, or brandish props; his authority lies in unveiled Scripture and Spirit-impelled conviction. Still, clarity demands specificity: describe the loneliness of outer darkness, the irrevocability of divine sentence, the regret of squandered mercies. Avoid cartoonish exaggerations that make hell a carnival of demons; portray it as Jesus did—"weeping and gnashing of teeth." Sensory language—silence after the gavel, door slammed by the master—can jolt the complacent awake. Yet each description should serve redemption, not morbid curiosity. Test the illustration: does it magnify the horror of being cut off from God or merely entertain? If the latter, scrap it. Soul-shaking rhetoric is sober, not sensational.

11.3.2 Appeals to conscience: tapping the moral law written on every heart (Rom 2 :15)

Paul leveraged Athenians' altar "to the unknown god" as a bridge to their suppressed knowledge. Modern preachers likewise press the universal instinct for justice. Ask listeners why betrayal wounds, why outrage erupts at trafficking. Having surfaced conscience, show how each transgression—white lies, porn clicks—breaks the same law they expect from others. Personalize with probing questions: "Would you be comfortable if your hidden thoughts were livestreamed this week?" Such appeals bypass intellectual smokescreens, aiming at the moral nerve where guilt resides. When conscience nods, the preacher can unveil Christ as the only antidote that satisfies both justice and mercy, sealing the argument with Romans 2 :16: God will judge secrets by Jesus.

11.3.3 Proper use of emotion—pathos that serves truth, not manipulation

Emotion is the bloodstream of persuasion; without it sermons remain cadavers of bare facts. Yet ethical rhetoric refuses manipulation—manufactured tears, melodramatic pauses timed to background keys. Instead, the preacher allows his own heart to be genuinely moved by the text; unfeigned earnestness radiates. Variation in voice—soft lament when exposing sin's damage, firm resolve when announcing judgment, jubilant lift when unveiling grace—mirrors textual contours. Eye contact, open posture, and pace slow enough for weighty lines to land all respect hearers' dignity. If emotion arises, it supports logos (content) and ethos (character), forging trust. Congregants sense the difference between contrived intensity and Spirit-kindled compassion. The former manipulates; the latter melts resistance.

11.3.4 Christ-centered climax: terror relieved only by the bleeding Lamb

Every sermon must sprint to Golgotha or leave souls bleeding on Sinai. The preacher, having raised thunderheads of wrath, now parts clouds to reveal the cross. Detail substitution: sins transferred, righteousness imputed. Invite with immediacy—"Today, if you hear His voice…"—and sufficiency—"whoever comes, He will never cast out." Emphasize exclusivity without apology: no refuge outside the Savior. Employ testimonies—a former addict, a self-righteous elder brother—to prove the Lamb's wide embrace. Close with concrete calls: repent, believe, be baptized, seek counsel. Let final sentences echo grace: "Flee to Him now; the storm has fallen on His shoulders so it need never fall on yours." Listeners should leave the sanctuary seeing blood-stained wood towering over yawning pits of judgment—one path of escape, gloriously open.

11.4 Pastoral Tone: Severity Tempered with Tears

11.4.1 Voice, pace, and body language that convey earnest love

An urgent message delivered coldly can freeze hearts; severity requires a thermostat of compassion. Voice volume may surge on key indictments but must soften when offering mercy. Pace slows on weighty warnings, giving consciences time to echo; it quickens with gospel excitement. Gestures stay open-handed rather than finger-pointing, signaling invitation over accusation. Facial expression matters: brows knit in grief, not scorn; eyes wet, not detached. Such embodied empathy convinces hearers that the preacher longs for their rescue, not their humiliation. Paul spoke "with tears" (Acts 20 :31); so should we.

11.4.2 Weeping prophets and apostles—the authority of compassion (Luke 19 :41)

Jesus wept over the city that would crucify Him; Jeremiah's eyes were fountains for a rebellious nation (Jer 9 :1). Their tears authenticate their warnings. When congregants see genuine anguish, suspicion of manipulation evaporates. They grasp that the preacher has first applied the sermon to himself. This authority of compassion cannot be faked; it springs from secret prayer, meditating on hell and cross until heart muscles ache. Such preachers can speak of wrath without relish and of grace with unembarrassed delight. The combination disarms cynics and woos sinners.

11.4.3 Public prayer that owns the preacher's own need of grace

After proclamation, intercession models response. The minister confesses corporate and personal sin, kneels (literally or figuratively), and pleads the merits of Christ. He names specific idolatries—greed in our budgets, voyeurism in our screens—and seeks cleansing. This transparency collapses pew-pulpit distance: all stand level at the cross. Assurance of pardon follows, read aloud from promises like Isaiah 55 :6-7. Such liturgical ownership prevents the sermon from sounding like a prosecutor's indictment; instead, it becomes a family conversation led by an older brother who knows the Father's heart.

11.4.4 After-sermon care: counseling seekers and soothing the wounded conscience

Awakening sermons stir emotions that require shepherding. Pastors linger after dismissal, elders station themselves for prayer, and trained counselors watch for distraught newcomers. They answer questions, clarify doctrine, and distinguish conviction from condemnation. Resources— booklets on assurance, sign-ups for baptism class—are readily available. Follow-up visits ensure that initial tears produce lasting fruit. The goal is midwifery: helping spiritual births progress safely into newborn discipleship. Neglecting this stage squanders harvest; embracing it completes the ministry of terror mingled with mercy.

11.5 Translating Terror and Mercy Across Cultures and Generations

11.5.1 Preaching wrath in a therapeutic age—framing justice without caricature

Late-modern societies prize self-esteem and pathologize guilt, so the preacher must unwrap divine wrath as moral realism, not cosmic tantrum. He can begin with injustices everyone laments—genocide, child abuse, predatory lending—showing that moral outrage presupposes an ultimate Judge who shares, even surpasses, our concern (Gen 18 :25). By tracing suffering to sin's vandalism, he reframes wrath as love's necessary opposition to evil, not the negation of love. Careful exegesis of Romans 1 :18-32 exposes the passive dimension of judgment—God "giving over" rebels to self-chosen ruin— before progressing to the active sentence of Romans 2 :5. Contemporary metaphors help: a surgeon who hates cancer or a judge who hates trafficking. Such images defuse caricatures of a trigger-happy deity while preserving holy severity. Once listeners grasp that wrath safeguards the cosmos, mercy shines brighter as the costly way God can stay just while justifying sinners (Rom 3 :26). The preacher thereby honors modern sensitivities to love without surrendering biblical thunder.

11.5.2 Addressing pluralistic listeners—exclusivity of Christ with humble boldness

In plural societies absolutist claims sound intolerant, yet Acts 4 :12 still asserts "no other name." The key is posture: proclaim exclusivity as rescued beggars recommending the only bread they've found, not as tribal winners keeping rivals out. Historical facts—the resurrection's empty tomb, eyewitness testimony (1 Cor 15 :3-8)—anchor the claim in public events rather than private preference. Logical coherence follows: if sin is cosmic treason, only a divine-human Mediator can pay infinite debt and represent finite rebels (1 Tim 2 :5). Humility admits Christians often wielded exclusivity as a cudgel; boldness still invites hearers to weigh Jesus' credentials above competing gurus. Dialogical Q&A after sermons, apologetics courses, and book clubs with seekers embody respectful engagement. Listeners discover that Christian particularism is not cultural chauvinism but a global offer from a crucified Savior who purchased people from every tribe (Rev 5 :9).

11.5.3 Digital and social-media pulpit: clips, podcasts, and the risk of sound-bite outrage

Streaming platforms amplify sermons beyond church walls, but algorithms reward outrage clips stripped from context. Wise preachers therefore craft digital excerpts that retain both halves of the message—ninety seconds on sin followed by ninety on grace—so viewers encounter the antidote alongside the diagnosis. Show notes can link to full sermons, transcripts, and pastoral resources for wounded consciences. Social posts should eschew click-bait headlines that trivialize hell or sentimentalize grace; instead they summarize biblical claims and invite dialogue. Moderating comment threads with patience (2 Tim 2 :24-25) prevents flame wars from discrediting the gospel. Short-form video testimonies—"I once scoffed at judgment, but mercy found me"—humanize doctrine for scrolling skeptics. Digital analytics help gauge reach but must never eclipse faithfulness; a viral clip that outruns pastoral care courts spiritual casualties. In every medium, the preacher's aim matches Paul's: "by all means save some" (1 Cor 9 :22).

11.5.4 Multilingual and multicultural considerations—images that travel, idioms that don't

Fire, chains, and courtrooms resonate differently in shame-honor or animist cultures. Translators and indigenous leaders can suggest metaphors—defilement cleansed or clan debts canceled—that carry equivalent moral weight. Avoid idioms like "hit the road, Jack" that baffle non-Western ears. In oral cultures, narrative sermons tracing Joseph's betrayal and reconciliation communicate terror and mercy experientially, while literate settings may prefer logical exposition. Hand gestures, eye contact, and pacing adjust to audience norms: a Western pause for reflection may read as uncertainty elsewhere. Employing bilingual slides or audio ensures listeners grasp both the warning and the invitation. Above all, keep the cross central; the imagery may vary, but Christ crucified remains the power of God and wisdom of God for every ethnicity (1 Cor 1 :23-24).

11.6 Congregational Ecosystems That Sustain Law-and-Gospel Preaching

11.6.1 Liturgy that progresses from confession to assurance every Sunday

A gospel-shaped order of service rehearses redemptive flow: call to worship, confession, lament, assurance, thanksgiving, Word, Table, benediction. Each element echoes terror or mercy so congregants feel the rhythm weekly. Public confession passages like Psalm 51 awaken conscience; absolution texts such as Isaiah 55 :7 comfort it. Even children learn the pattern—sin is serious, grace is greater. Rotating historic creeds anchors emotions in doctrinal ballast. Anthem selections range from "Dies Irae"–inspired verses to "Amazing Grace," displaying full emotional spectrum. Over time, this liturgical catechesis prepares hearts to receive awakening sermons without whiplash because the congregation already lives within a law-gospel dialect.

11.6.2 Small-group rhythms of mutual exhortation following awakening sermons

House gatherings the week after a weighty sermon offer space to process conviction and celebrate hope. Leaders open with Scripture, invite honest sharing—What sins surfaced? What aspects of Christ's work encouraged you?—

and guide prayer of repentance and faith. Accountability partners may set concrete goals: reconcile with a coworker, install accountability software, schedule a counseling appointment. Facilitators resist both extremes: allowing despair to linger without gospel or permitting jokes that deflect conviction. By revisiting the sermon's dual edge in relational settings, the church turns monologue into dialogue, reinforcing transformation.

11.6.3 Sacraments as tactile reinforcement of wrath averted and grace bestowed

Baptism dramatizes death under judgment waters and resurrection into mercy (Rom 6 :3-4). Candidates share testimonies that name past rebellion and present rescue, giving the congregation fresh visual theology. The Lord's Supper weekly (or monthly) shows wrath exhausted on the broken body and blood, yet communion implies fellowship restored. Fencing the table—warning unrepentant guests—preserves gravity; open invitation to all believers preserves grace. Children's questions—Why blood? Why bread?—become teachable moments about holiness and forgiveness. Thus the ordinary means of grace anchor the extraordinary claims of preaching in tangible practices.

11.6.4 Seasons of prayer and fasting that soften soil for convicting proclamation

Historic awakenings were preceded by concerted intercession—Methodist class-meeting vigils, Korean dawn prayers. Congregations today schedule 24-hour prayer chains or quarterly fast days pleading for soft hearts and bold preaching (Ezek 36 :37). Prayer guides include confession of communal sins—apathy, consumerism—and petitions for softened visitors. Fasting attunes appetites to spiritual hunger, making souls more receptive when sermons cut deep. Post-fast testimony nights record answered prayers: prodigals attending, marriages restored, baptisms scheduled. This culture of supplication breaks the fallow ground so the blade of conviction enters without bouncing off hardened soil.

183

11.7 The Preacher's Life: Credibility Through Consecration

11.7.1 Private holiness and secret prayer as the furnace of public urgency

No homiletical polish compensates for thin communion with God. Jesus withdrew to lonely places (Mark 1 :35); Edwards rode into Northampton woods for solitary intercession. Daily disciplines—Scripture meditation, journaling, repentance—forge a soul that feels eternity. Urgency springs from hours gazing at the coming throne, not from caffeine or deadlines. Hidden victories over lust or envy give moral authority when calling others to repent. Conversely, secret compromise siphons anointing; words become tin echoes. The preacher's first congregation is the heart; from its overflow the mouth speaks (Luke 6 :45).

11.7.2 Humility formed by continual awareness of personal deliverance from wrath

Paul never strayed far from "chief of sinners" (1 Tim 1 :15). Remembering deserved damnation prevents a judgmental tone. Pastors recount their conversion in sermons and counseling, not spotlighting themselves but magnifying grace. They seek feedback, admit mistakes publicly, and credit team members, modeling the gospel they preach. Humility keeps terror and mercy balanced: stern against sin, gentle with sinners. Congregations sense authenticity and listen when such shepherds warn.

11.7.3 Suffering and simplicity—embodied proofs that eternity, not comfort, rules the heart

Affliction—illness, bereavement, slander—burns dross from rhetoric. A sufferer speaking of future wrath and glory sounds believable, like a man who has peeked beyond the veil (2 Cor 4 :17-18). Voluntary simplicity likewise undercuts accusations of profiteering: modest lifestyle, transparent finances, generosity toward missions. These choices whisper, "My treasure is elsewhere." The preacher who declines luxury preaching circuits to shepherd funerals at home nails credibility that marketing budgets cannot buy.

11.7.4 Accountability structures that guard against hypocrisy and burnout

Plural elder teams share preaching load, review sermons, and monitor conduct. Annual retreats include confession sessions; outside mentors ask blunt questions about screen habits and marriage health. Mental-health rests every seven years prevent adrenalized ministries from flaming out. Congregations pray weekly for leaders' holiness, recognizing the enemy's bullseye. Such structures fence the messenger so the message remains untarnished; they also free the preacher to thunder and weep without fear of hidden scandal detonating tomorrow.

Conclusion

Preaching that merely informs minds or entertains emotions is too light for the freight of eternity. Heaven and hell hang in the balance when the Word is opened. The God who flung stars into space and hung His Son upon a cross has entrusted clay vessels with a message as sharp as lightning and as sweet as honey. To discharge that trust we must warn with watchman's urgency and woo with Bridegroom's tenderness, keeping severity and kindness in irrevocable union (Rom 11 :22). The results belong to the Spirit, but the faithfulness belongs to us. May every reader who climbs a pulpit or shares a testimony feel the blood-earnest thrill of bearing two treasures: a vial of holy fire and a cup of living water. Spend them both—empty the vial to expose sin's peril, pour the water to quench sin's thirst—and you will hear on that final day, "Well done, good and faithful servant."

Chapter 12. Hope Beyond Judgment: The Grand Finale

Christian hope is not a bright ribbon tied around a grim future; it is the future itself—hard-won, blood-bought, and already breaking into the present for everyone hidden in Christ. Throughout this book we have traced humanity's peril under divine wrath, the refuge offered at the cross, and the marks of a life transformed. Yet the gospel symphony would end in a minor key if it stopped at personal regeneration. Scripture insists that the God who justifies individuals also intends to rehabilitate the cosmos, to vindicate justice publicly, and to serenade redeemed multitudes with a song no sorrow can mute. The final vision is therefore neither universal doom nor bland cloudbound repose, but a resurrected earth ablaze with holy delight—a realm where wrath has finished its cleansing work and grace floresces without competition (Rev 21:1-4). Holding that finale in view changes everything: grief acquires an expiration date, persistence gains purpose, purity becomes plausible, and mission pulses with fresh urgency. This chapter explores that grand horizon in seven movements, showing how judgment's fire births creation's dawn and how believers should live with one foot already planted in tomorrow's world. Along the way we will confront common caricatures—annihilated universes, sterile eternity, reward-earning pride—and replace them with the Bible's rich tapestry of renewal, banquet, vocation, and unending wonder. May the vista ahead lift drooping heads, steady wobbly knees, and propel each reader to echo the church's oldest longing: *Marana tha—Come, Lord Jesus* (1 Cor 16:22).

Prelude - The Dawn After the Deluge

Why Christian hope must look past wrath to promised renewal (Rom 8:18-25)

Paul admits creation now groans, marred by futility, yet he refuses despair because the present sufferings "are not worth comparing with the glory that is to be revealed" (Rom 8:18). His logic hinges on sequence: wrath and decay are real but penultimate; liberation and glory are definitive. The Spirit's firstfruits in believers—love rising where hatred ruled, peace germinating in anxious soil—function as down-payments of that cosmic harvest. If hope focused only on escaping punishment, it would encourage bunker spirituality; but hope that anticipates a renewed universe emboldens cultural engagement and ecological stewardship even as we await consummation. Just as a sunrise guarantees the retreat of night, God's oath of new creation guarantees that wrath's darkness cannot last. Therefore Christian eschatology gazes beyond the tempest to the emerging horizon, declaring with Isaiah that "the former things shall not be remembered" in the joy of remade heavens and earth (Isa 65:17). Without such forward sight, faith shrivels into stoic survival; with it, endurance flowers into eager expectation.

From furnace to feast—how judgment paves the way for joy (Isa 35:1-10)

Biblical storytellers often pair images of smelting and celebration: ore enters a blazing furnace only to emerge as glittering gold, and deserts burst into bloom once scorching judgment passes (Isa 35:1-2). God's wrath is thus not the sadistic opposite of joy but the surgical prerequisite, excising evil so that gladness may safely root. Egypt's plagues shattered oppressive chains; Sinai's quaking birthed covenant intimacy; Calvary's darkness heralded resurrection dawn. In the final reckoning, cosmic fire will incinerate everything hostile to love, leaving a purified arena where "the ransomed of the LORD shall return...and sorrow and sighing shall flee away" (Isa 35:10). Grasping that sequence reorients lament: believers weep over injustice yet anticipate its irreversible eviction. Likewise, evangelism becomes an invitation not merely to dodge flames but to join an eternal banquet already prepared (Matt 22:1-10). Judgment, then, is mercy's bulldozer—clearing rubble so the palace of shalom can rise.

Previewing the last movement in the symphony of redemption

Every symphony reprises earlier motifs before its finale, resolving tension in climactic harmony. Genesis introduced Eden's garden, priest-king vocation, serpent menace, and shattered fellowship. History replayed these themes—tabernacle hinting at Eden's presence, David prefiguring royal rule, prophets foreseeing serpent's demise—yet the chords resolved only partially. Revelation's closing pages bring full resolution: garden becomes garden-city, fellowship widens to innumerable nations, and the dragon is hurled into irreversible exile (Rev 20:10; 22:1-5). Chapter 12 will trace that consummation under seven headings: the recreated cosmos, the public verdict, the marriage feast, the restored shalom, the spectrum of rewards, the beatific vision, and the present implications. Each movement will open a window onto the landscape awaiting God's children, not for speculative timelines but for anchored hope. Like travelers cresting a ridge to glimpse home's lights, we will survey the destination that renders every valley worthwhile.

12.1 The Eschatological Promise: New Heavens and New Earth

12.1.1 Isaiah's prophetic seed and Peter's apostolic harvest (Isa 65:17; 2 Pet 3:13)

Centuries before Christ, Isaiah heard God pledge, "Behold, I create new heavens and a new earth," a promise so staggering that Israel's post-exilic struggles could not exhaust its scope (Isa 65:17). The Hebrew verb *bara'* echoes Genesis 1, signaling not mere repair but divine creativity unleashed anew. Yet Isaiah also depicts recognizable continuity—homes built, vineyards enjoyed—hinting that the future world will retain creaturely textures purified, not discarded (Isa 65:21-22). Peter picks up that seed and waters it with gospel clarity: after the present heavens and earth are refined by fire, believers "are waiting for new heavens and a new earth in which righteousness dwells" (2 Pet 3:13). The Greek *kainos* ("new in quality") reinforces renewal rather than replacement. Thus the biblical story rejects both nihilistic extinction and Platonic escape, promising instead a resurrected cosmos where righteousness feels as natural as breathing. This continuity grounds Christian investment in culture and conservation: what we fashion for God's glory today foreshadows treasures kings will bring into the Lamb's city (Rev 21:24-26).

12.1.2 Cosmic fire as purifying, not annihilating—renewal through refining (Mal 3:2-3)

Apocalyptic fire texts often spark annihilationist readings, yet prophetic imagery clarifies purpose: the Refiner sits over the crucible until dross floats away, leaving silver gleaming (Mal 3:2-3). Paul likewise compares judgment day to flames testing each work's quality; what is combustible burns, what is precious survives (1 Cor 3:13-15). Peter's "elements dissolved" phrase (2 Pet 3:10) likely envisions cosmic deconstruction akin to Noah's deluge—devastating yet not obliterative (cf. 3:6). Fire, then, is catalytic, not terminal. Believers therefore anticipate continuity of identity and artistry through the flames; Bach's fugues, when offered for Christ, may echo in transfigured acoustics. Understanding refining fire also tempers ecological despair: while human sin scars the planet, God's furnace will cleanse toxins more thoroughly than any environmental policy, ensuring creation's sigh becomes song (Rom 8:21).

12.1.3 Continuity and discontinuity between present and future creation

New-creation theology balances sameness and surprise: Jesus' risen body still bore nail prints yet walked through walls; so the renewed earth will retain mountains yet radiate with unobstructed glory. Continuity preserves creaturely identity— languages, memories, cultural accomplishments—allowing personal stories to thread into eternity's tapestry (Rev 7:9). Discontinuity eliminates death, disease, and decay, introducing capacities we cannot fathom: perhaps interstellar exploration without fear, creativity without critique, technology without tyranny. This framework corrects two errors: escapist spirituality that despises materiality, and utopian activism expecting Eden before the King's return. Instead, Christians labor now as apprentices laying tiles that the Master Builder will incorruptibly set into New Jerusalem's floor.

12.1.4 Ecological and vocational implications of coming restoration

If God intends to rehabilitate the biosphere, Christians cannot treat creation as disposable packaging. Recycling, habitat restoration, and sustainable business become acts of eschatological witness, not political fashion. Likewise, vocational callings—coding software, curing diseases, composing symphonies—acquire eternal hue. Because labor in the Lord is "not in vain" (1 Cor 15:58), efforts toward beauty, order, and justice anticipate kingdom realities. Farmers nurturing soil, teachers awakening curiosity, and entrepreneurs solving poverty preview a world where thorns no longer sabotage harvests (Rev 22:3). Knowing that final hope is corporate and cosmic liberates believers from self-centered escapism and commissions them as ambassadors of the future in the present.

12.2 Final Justification and Public Vindication

12.2.1 The open verdict—private acquittal declared before the universe (Matt 25 :34)

The instant a sinner trusts Christ, God the Judge issues a hidden verdict of "righteous" in the courtroom of heaven (Rom 5 :1). At the last day that private acquittal will become a public proclamation before angels, demons, and the watching nations. Jesus' parable of the sheep and goats pictures the King announcing, "Come, you who are blessed of my Father, inherit the kingdom" (Matt 25 :34). This is not a second justification earned by works; it is the unveiling of the first, evidenced by Spirit-produced deeds (Eph 2 :10). Public affirmation silences every accusation—satanic, societal, or self-inflicted—because the Judge Himself confesses the believer's name (Rev 3 :5). In that moment the world will finally see what God already declared in secret: that weak, limping saints were, all along, robed in the righteousness of Christ. Such future recognition infuses present obscurity with dignity; unnoticed acts of faithfulness will one day echo through the cosmos.

12.2.2 Books opened, names confessed—why God goes public (Rev 20 :11-15)

John sees books of deeds and a separate "book of life." The dual record underscores both perfect justice and lavish mercy: every work matters, yet rescue rests on the Lamb's ledger. Public disclosure vindicates God's governance, demonstrating that no hidden atrocity escaped His notice (Eccl 12 :14). It also vindicates believers who were slandered or martyred; the courtroom reveals their obedience and the world's injustice (Rev 6 :9-11). Far from shaming redeemed sinners, this exposure magnifies grace, for the very sins once crimson are now bleached by Christ's blood (Isa 1 :18). The transparency answers centuries of "How long, O Lord?" and fuels eternal gratitude. Knowing that secrets will surface prompts present integrity and relentless repentance (1 Tim 5 :24-25).

12.2.3 Answering the problem of deferred justice—saints vindicated, evil exposed

Temporal history often ends with tyrants in tombs of honor and victims in unmarked graves. The final assize overturns such mockeries: Lazarus is comforted, the rich man tormented (Luke 16 :25). Holocaust architects, unrepentant traffickers, and quiet abusers will confront irrefutable evidence—no plea bargains, no technicalities. Conversely, maligned missionaries, whistle-blowers, and single parents who clung to Christ will hear public commendation. This prospect satisfies the longing of every oppressed heart without inviting vigilantism; vengeance belongs to God, not man (Rom 12 :19). It also relativizes earthly verdicts—court acquittals of the guilty or convictions of the righteous—assuring believers that ultimate justice is pending. Such assurance sustains costly obedience when outcomes appear lopsided now.

12.2.4 Pastoral comfort: sufferers celebrated, oppressors silenced

For trauma survivors, the promise of divine exposure brings healing: their story will be heard by the One whose eyes are like fire (Rev 1 :14). No gaslighting abuser can revise the record; the Judge saw every blow and will reckon every tear. Congregants enduring ridicule for holiness can persevere, knowing Jesus will one day "praise" what is done in secret (1 Cor 4 :5). Pastors apply this hope at sickbeds and funerals—

"Your labor is not in vain" (1 Cor 15 :58). The same hope warns oppressors in the pew: hidden porn, racism, or fraud will appear unless covered now by Christ's atonement. Thus final vindication is both pillow and prod—comforting the wounded, unsettling the unrepentant—until mercy closes every open case.

12.3 The Marriage Supper of the Lamb

12.3.1 Covenant climax—betrothal consummated in glory (Rev 19 :6-9)

Redemptive history is a love story moving from betrothal at Sinai to consummation in the New Jerusalem. John hears thunderous praise announcing, "The marriage of the Lamb has come," and angelic hosts pronounce the blessedness of those invited (Rev 19 :7-9). The imagery fulfills Old-Testament promises of Yahweh as bridegroom (Hos 2 :19-20) and Jesus' self-identification in Galilee (Mark 2 :19). Earthly weddings echo this cosmic union, but the final ceremony lacks end or shadow. Legal status (justification) flowers into experiential intimacy; faith gives way to sight, and distance collapses into embrace. Every ache for relational wholeness finds answer at this table where Love incarnate presides.

12.3.2 Table fellowship renewed: Eden's lost banquet, Isaiah's foretold feast

Human history began with shared fruit in a garden and fractured when that fellowship broke. Isaiah foresaw God preparing "a feast of rich food" that would swallow death (Isa 25 :6-8). Jesus previewed that feast feeding multitudes and sharing Passover wine, pledging not to drink again until the kingdom comes (Luke 22 :16-18). The Supper today is therefore both memorial and appetizer, sustaining longing for the full banquet. At the Lamb's table, hunger ends, loneliness evaporates, and global enemies become seat-mates redeemed by the same blood. Meals on missionary fields and potlucks in church basements foreshadow that day, practicing inclusivity that will be perfected in glory.

12.3.3 Garments of righteousness—imputed and perfected (Rev 19 :8)

The bride's linen is "bright and pure," identified as "the righteous deeds of the saints" yet granted, not earned. This paradox captures forensic justification (linen given) and Spirit-empowered sanctification (linen woven through deeds, Phil 2 :12-13). No unclean stain mars the fabric; Christ loved the church and washed her to present "without spot or wrinkle" (Eph 5 :27). Weddings obliterate memories of courtship stumbles; likewise, glorification erases every lingering blemish. The sight of the church dazzling in borrowed splendor will silence all proud boasting and all self-loathing, leaving only grateful adoration.

12.3.4 Missional invite—"Blessed are those called to the supper"

The angel's beatitude in Revelation 19 doubles as global invitation. Evangelism is essentially handing out wedding invitations sealed in Christ's blood. The guest list spans tribes, tongues, and tax brackets; none are too stained if they embrace the dress code of grace (Matt 22 :11-14). Missionaries translate menus into thousands of languages, ensuring every palate hears of rich fare. Hospitality on earth— open tables for students, refugees, skeptics—visually extend that eschatological RSVP. Refusal has eternal consequence, but acceptance costs only pride and unbelief. The church's joy today advertises the feast tomorrow; sullen saints are poor recruiters, but satisfied saints compel attendance.

12.4 Restored Creation: Shalom Recovered

12.4.1 No more curse—thorns, pain, and death reversed (Rev 22 :3)

John's final vista states tersely, "No longer will there be anything accursed." The Edenic malediction—thorny ground, sweaty toil, childbirth agony, looming mortality (Gen 3 :16-19)—is lifted. Agriculture flourishes without drought; bodies thrive without disease; relationships flourish without fear. Isaiah envisions elderly sinners reaching a hundred years, a poetic way of saying death's dominion collapses (Isa 65 :20). Paul calls death "the last enemy" to be destroyed (1 Cor 15 :26); its funeral signals shalom's enthronement. Hymns of lament retire forever; tears become museum relics God himself wipes away (Rev 21 :4).

12.4.2 Harmonized relationships—human, angelic, animal, and divine (Isa 11 :6-9)

Wolf and lamb sharing pasture symbolize more than zoological peace; they depict every rivalry dissolved under Messiah's reign. Social hierarchies warped by sin—racial hostility, class arrogance, gender warfare—heal into mutual honor (Gal 3 :28). Angels and humans engage without fear; demons are exiled, leaving only holy companionship. Work teams, choirs, research guilds may include both human and seraphic members exploring God's wisdom together (Eph 3 :10). The earth will finally be "full of the knowledge of the LORD as waters cover the sea" (Isa 11 :9), saturating every interaction with sacramental awe.

12.4.3 Cultural treasures of the nations brought into the Holy City (Rev 21 :24-26)

John sees kings streaming to New Jerusalem bearing the "glory and honor of the nations." God's plan never scrapped culture; it purifies and re-presents it. African rhythms, Asian calligraphy, European cathedrals, and indigenous storytelling may all enter, freed from idolatry. This influx fulfills Haggai's vision of the desired treasures filling God's house (Hag 2 :7). Mission work that dignifies local arts now is rehearsal for that parade. Xenophobia finds no foothold when every ethnic gift adorns the Bride's city.

12.4.4 Endless exploration—eternity as dynamic, not static, delight

New creation is not an eternal church service frozen in one climactic chord; it is an ever-unfolding adventure with God as tour guide. Revelation's imagery of kings reigning "for ever and ever" (Rev 22 :5) suggests governance, discovery, and creativity. Finite minds will forever mine infinite glory—mathematicians probing new theorems, artists unveiling fresh hues, scientists naming star clusters God never let telescopes see. Every discovery becomes fresh doxology, echoing Psalm 111 :2: "Great are the works of the LORD, studied by all who delight in them." Joy will not plateau because the object of joy is inexhaustible. As horizons expand, so will capacity for wonder, ensuring that the flame of delight never flickers.

12.5 Eternal Rewards and Degrees of Glory

12.5.1 Crowns promised: life, righteousness, glory, rejoicing (Jas 1 :12; 2 Tim 4 :8)

The New Testament scatters reward imagery like jewels across its pages, naming specific "crowns" that Christ will bestow. James promises the "crown of life" to saints who persevere under trial, signaling vitality that suffering could not snuff (Jas 1 :12). Paul awaits the "crown of righteousness," anticipating the moment when imputed righteousness flowers into perfected character (2 Tim 4 :8). Peter speaks of the "crown of glory" for faithful shepherds (1 Pet 5 :4), while Thessalonian converts themselves become Paul's "crown of rejoicing" (1 Thess 2 :19). These metaphors assure believers that earthly losses will be overcompensated by divine honor. Each crown, though varied, centers on the Giver's delight, not the recipient's bragging rights. The diversity of reward underscores God's personal knowledge—He tailors commendation to specific obedience. Such specificity motivates endurance: the persecuted picture life-crowns, teachers picture glory-crowns, evangelists picture rejoicing-crowns. Hope thus becomes concrete enough to steel weak knees today.

12.5.2 Varying capacities for joy—star differs from star (1 Cor 15 :41-42)

Paul likens resurrected bodies to celestial bodies, each "star differing from star in glory." By analogy, believers will share equal title to eternal life yet enjoy differing capacities for joy based on Spirit-formed faithfulness. Jonathan Edwards compared this to vessels of different sizes all brimming to the top—each full, none envious, yet distinct in volume. Jesus' parable of minas echoes the theme: faithful servants rule over ten or five cities according to stewardship (Luke 19 :17-19). This prospect converts mundane choices—quiet intercession, unseen generosity—into everlasting gain. It also exposes cheap-grace passivity; saved souls can still "suffer loss" when wood-hay stubble burns (1 Cor 3 :15). Yet heavenly inequality induces no jealousy, because self-centeredness has died; each saint delights in every other's capacity as orchestra members thrill at the whole symphony. Thus rewarding differentiation magnifies grace, not merit, displaying what God can weave from yielded lives.

12.5.3 Faithfulness in "little" stewardships magnified forever (Luke 19 :17)

Jesus labels the servant's original mina "very little," yet its prudent use yields city-wide authority. The ratio is absurdly gracious—ten-fold, even five-fold returns—signaling disproportionate reward. Every diaper changed in Jesus' name or spreadsheet scrutinized for ethical compliance is seed sown for eternal oversight. Such logic dignifies the ordinary; believers need not chase public platforms to secure future largeness. Conversely, neglect of modest duties reveals distrust in the Master's generosity and squanders kingdom opportunity. This calculus frees disciples to focus on faithfulness, leaving scale with God. When the kingdom dawns, seemingly backstage saints may govern galaxies, proving that obscurity on earth can translate into cosmic prominence. Therefore, "whatever you do," however small, "do all in the name of the Lord" (Col 3 :17), expecting exponential reversal at the audit of grace.

12.5.4 Safeguarding grace—rewards as gifts, not wages (Rev 4 :10)

John sees elders casting crowns before the throne, dramatizing that rewards ultimately redound to God's glory (Rev 4 :10-11). Even crowns are byproducts of grace: God "works in us" the very deeds He later praises (Phil 2 :13). Thus rewards neither inflate pride nor jeopardize justification; they are celebratory gifts from Father to child, not salaries owed to employees. This frame guards against both legalism ("earn heaven") and apathy ("rewards don't matter"). When saints present crowns back to Christ, the exchange becomes a liturgy of love—He honors them, they honor Him, happiness circulates. Understanding this cycle fuels service without panic: effort matters, but its success rests on Spirit-empowered enablement. Believers labor, yet grace reigns from first desire to final accolade.

12.6 Unending Worship and the Beatific Vision

12.6.1 Seeing God in the face of Christ—ultimate satisfaction (Rev 22 :4)

John's climactic promise—"They will see his face"—fulfills centuries of holy longing (Rev 22 :4). Moses glimpsed only God's back (Ex 33 :23); Isaiah feared disintegration at a throne vision (Isa 6 :5). The beatific vision grants what sin once forbade: direct, unmarred fellowship with Triune beauty mediated through the glorified humanity of Jesus. Augustine wrote, "You have made us for Yourself, and our heart is restless until it rests in You"; that rest culminates here. Such sight satisfies intellect (truth embodied), emotion (love reciprocated), and will (purpose completed). No boredom intrudes because finite minds cannot exhaust infinite glory; every gaze reveals new facets of holiness and tenderness. This prospect reframes all earthly pleasures as appetizers and renders idol worship absurd—why bow to trinkets when the Source of splendor awaits?

12.6.2 Worship as work and play—service that feels like song (Rev 7 :15)

Revelation blends priestly language ("serve him day and night") with festive song, showing that heavenly worship is active, not sedentary (Rev 7 :15). The curse lifted, labor no longer scratches thorns; vocation becomes melodic. Gardeners cultivate orchids that never wilt, scientists decode nebulae's secrets as acts of praise, and rulers administer justice without lobbying corruption. C.S. Lewis captured this fusion: "Joy is the serious business of heaven." Play also finds rightful place—laughter rings across golden streets, games without envy entertain. Sabbath and vocation meld, abolishing the toil-leisure dichotomy that plagues fallen rhythms. Thus eternal worship is holistic human flourishing—mind, body, society—throbbing in sync with the Lamb's heart.

12.6.3 Ever-expanding wonder—finite saints, infinite glory

Because God's attributes are inexhaustible, worship must be exploratory. Ephesians 2 :7 envisions God "showing the immeasurable riches of his grace...in the coming ages," plural, implying successive unveilings. Imagine an unending museum where every corridor opens to ten more, each artifact reflecting aspects of divine creativity—mathematical elegance, comedic timing, subatomic symmetry. Saints will dialogue with archangels and patriarchs, sharing insights without rivalry. The Holy Spirit, eternal tour guide, will orchestrate these discoveries, ensuring that awe never plateaus into familiarity. Therefore, hope for heaven need not fear monotony; delight will deepen as capacity grows, like climbing a mountain range discovering higher peaks beyond every summit.

12.6.4 The harmony of nations—multilingual hallelujahs (Rev 5 :9-13)

John's throne room resounds with a song "in every language," proving that Pentecost's reversal of Babel reaches consummation. Cultures retain distinct timbres—drums, flutes, tonal scales—yet blend into one global anthem. Lyrics revolve around the Lamb's ransom "from every tribe," so diversity exalts the breadth of grace. Racial strife, genocides, and colonial wounds are healed, not erased, as redeemed peoples testify how Christ entered their history. Mission today rehearses that chorus; when churches translate hymns into minority tongues, they anticipate heaven's soundtrack. Learning to celebrate cultural difference now trains hearts for eternal citizenship. Any form of ethnocentric superiority is therefore eschatologically obsolete.

12.7 Living Today in Light of the Finale

12.7.1 Steadfastness—"be immovable... your labor is not in vain" (1 Cor 15 :58)

Paul ends his resurrection chapter not with speculation but exhortation: knowing bodily renewal awaits, believers should throw themselves into "the work of the Lord." Martyrs endure flames, caregivers change diapers, scholars revise theses— all convinced effort echoes into eternity. Discouraged saints recall that setbacks are chapter breaks, not the epilogue. Perseverance manifests in daily plodding—quiet prayer, faithful commutes—confident seeds will sprout after the thaw. Thus eschatology fuels gritty faithfulness rather than escapist passivity.

12.7.2 Purity—everyone hoping in Him purifies himself (1 John 3 :2-3)

John links eschatological vision to ethical urgency: seeing future glory by faith ignites present cleansing. Just as a bride prepares for her wedding, the church jettisons bitterness, pornography, and greed that would clash with bridal linen. Purity is not prudishness but prophetic alignment—adopting kingdom culture ahead of schedule. Spiritual disciplines become wardrobe decisions fitting saints for tomorrow's banquet. Accountability friendships ask, "Does this habit belong in New Jerusalem?" and adjust course accordingly.

12.7.3 Hopeful realism—sorrowful yet rejoicing in a groaning world (2 Cor 6 :10)

Believers live between D-Day (resurrection) and V-Day (return), holding dual citizenship in suffering and glory. They weep at funerals without the sting of finality, protest injustice without cynicism, and age with dignity rather than despair. Hope grants permission to lament honestly because it forbids hopelessness. Christians model emotional breadth to a culture swinging between stoic denial and nihilistic panic. The Spirit's firstfruits enable simultaneous groaning and gratitude until adoption is complete (Rom 8 :23-25).

12.7.4 Proclamation—announcing the coming King while doors of mercy stand open

If a tsunami siren fails, coastal residents perish; likewise, silent churches betray neighbors destined for wrath. Because the Judge is also Savior, heralds can warn with tears and invite with joy. Every coffee-shop conversation, podcast episode, or missionary trek extends the wedding invitation before the banquet hall closes. Eschatology steels courage: mockery is momentary, souls are eternal. Believers thus engage culture, not retreat, confident that some listeners will hear the Spirit and join the global bride.

Conclusion

Wrath has marched through these pages like a purifying wildfire, and mercy has followed like spring bloom breaking from charred soil. The journey began with sinners dangling over flames and ends with saints dancing in a garden-city whose streets pulse with resurrected life. Between those poles stands the rugged cross—the hinge of history where terror met tenderness and holiness kissed sinners clean. Chapter 12 has widened the camera lens: judgment is not the story's period but its semicolon, after which God writes chapters of unending joy. New heavens and a new earth, public vindication, covenant banquet, restored shalom, tailored rewards, and the beatific vision compose a future too weighty for imagination yet too certain for doubt. Such hope forbids despair, fuels holiness, and galvanizes mission while the door of mercy still swings on grace-forged hinges. As you close this book, the final voice you hear is not Edwards's, nor mine, but Christ's: "Surely I am coming soon." May every reader answer with the only sentence that makes sense of everything now and everything next—"Amen. Come, Lord Jesus."

www.ingramcontent.com/pod-product-compliance
Lightning Source LLC
Chambersburg PA
CBHW060318050426
42449CB00011B/2545